'Ten years ago David Boddy thought that he must be mad to leap into headship from a career in business, and we thought that the governors must be mad to offer him the job; we were both wrong. He has not just rescued a school that had lost its way, but has made it an institution of stature, worth and individuality. Mr Boddy's opus on headship is imbued with his philosophy, and is written in management guru style - neither of which are naturally my territory, but neither of which I found distracting in the event. Fascinating, something to think quietly on, and something that ought not to be unique.'

    – Ralph Lucas
      Editor, *The Good Schools Guide*

To dearest Sue,

## Mɪɴᴅ Yᴏᴜʀ Hᴇᴀᴅ

and

keep inspiring all
who come into your
divine presence.

best wishes,

_David Dorrell_

# Mind Your Head

*An Emotional Intelligence Guide*
*for SCHOOL LEADERS*

## David Boddy

JOHN
CATT
EDUCATIONAL
LIMITED

*Mind Your Head: An Emotional Intelligence Guide to Surviving School Leadership* by David Boddy

Copyright © 2012 by David Boddy

ISBN: 978-1-908095-62-6

10 9 8 7 6 5 4 3 2 1

Printed and bound in the United Kingdom

Published by JOHN CATT Educational Limited and The Society of Heads
www.johncatt.com/
www.thesocietyofheads.org

Book Design by Jill Ronsley, Sun Editing & Book Design
www.suneditwrite.com

# Table of Contents

# About the Author

David Boddy was at first a reluctant head master. He came to the role after a life in journalism, politics, business and charity work.

His passion for more than 30 years has been philosophy and meditation. He has lectured widely on Advaita Vedanta, a key source of Eastern wisdom, and Platonic thought, both of which he regards as practical inspirations in leadership and daily life.

St James Senior Boys School is based in Ashford, Surrey. Meditation and philosophy are core aspects of the curriculum and school life.

He is a Trustee of the Education Renaissance Trust and Founder of the Lucca Leadership organisation, a world-wide charity for young people teaching community leadership skills.

He is married with three sons, six grandchildren (so far) and a belief that teaching, and headship is a God-calling.

In 2012 he was inaugurated Chairman of the Society of Heads.

# Acknowledgements

My thanks go to Peter Bodkin and colleagues at the Society of Heads, for their warmth of welcome, continued encouragement and willingness to lend their ears to a different approach to senior leadership in schools.

Thanks to my colleagues at St James Senior Boys who unwittingly have become the main characters in this book.

Thanks to Leon MacLaren, founder of both St James schools and the School of Economic Science, my first real teacher. Thanks to His Holiness Shri Shankararcharya Shantaananda Saraswati and Swami Shyam of the International Meditation Institute, Kullu, Himachal Pradesh, India; they filled my heart with love of Oneness and gave a language with which it could be expressed.

Thanks to my immediate crew for their loving support during this project, for their reading of drafts, typing of scripts and suggestions as to how to remove pomposity, arrogance and self-righteousness. Any of these qualities remaining in the book will show you how hard a job they have had. Particular thanks go to my editor, Jill Ronsley, whose wisdom shines through on every page and whose sharp editor's knife has ensured the text is far less wordy and much more readable.

Thanks to my loving wife and ever-supportive family and to those exceptionally close friends who don't see my faults and even if they do, graciously decide to ignore them.

# FOREWORD

DAVID BODDY'S APPROACH TO SCHOOL leadership refutes any assertions there may be that this topic has been exhausted. His offering is wonderfully refreshing, thought-provoking and most importantly, steeped in a personal self-reflective honesty which manages to offer advice without ever being patronising. It also offers both the experienced and the new head an opportunity to explore their own responses through a series of activities rooted in emotional intelligence at the end of every chapter.

As Margaret Thatcher's former political press secretary during her first two election campaigns and with no teaching experience in secondary education, David took a pathway to the headship of St James Senior Boys' School, an independent school in Ashford, Surrey, that would seem to most "career heads" unconventional. It is this very experience which makes his guide so engaging. He recounts with great integrity and humour the challenges he faced as a "reluctant head" at the start of his headship and how through self-reflection, self-analysis and meditation, he shaped the different constituents of the St James' community to live the values of their school. In so doing, his journey also provides us, at each stage, with stimulus to reflect on our own challenges, on what we can learn from our setbacks and how we can mould our individual leadership style to develop and sustain our performance.

Throughout this book, we are encouraged to challenge our experiences both as head teachers and more importantly as lead teachers, to educate and to inspire those whose lives we touch on a daily basis: our colleagues, our parents and first and foremost our pupils. At a time when recent governments, of all colours, continue to suffocate school leaders in a sea of bureaucratic initiatives, this book encourages our educational leaders to be adventurous, distinctive and above all independent. David Boddy's approach is light years away from the identikit taxonomy of skills which informs some of the current literature and national schemes on school leadership.

Whether you are considering becoming a head, or you are an experienced head in need of professional refreshment, whether you are in the maintained or independent sector, this highly personalised guide to the emotional intelligence of school leadership provides you with a very human and pragmatic approach to headship. It will also remind you that being a head teacher is more than just a job: it is a spiritual vocation.

– Gerry Holden

Chairman of the Professional Development
Committee of The Society of Heads

# INTRODUCTION

M

Y FIRST MENTOR, LEON MACLAREN, has a lot to answer for. He was my first real teacher. He knew things others didn't appear to know, and he was totally fearless when it came to proclaiming them. He couldn't abide 'experts' or religion but he did believe that humankind could be lifted out of its torpor and misery by the power of philosophy, or love of wisdom. He also had a knack for inspiring youngsters. I met him when I was twenty-one and worked with him until he died, twenty years later. Those of us who got to know him well picked up his belief that life had a purpose and that just a handful of young people, trained in wisdom, could create a renaissance and alter the world. He captivated my spirit, and ever since, whether working for a prime minister or leading a group of teachers as headmaster, I have sought to fulfil that vision.

When colleagues at The Society of Heads suggested I might write my own leadership story I was sceptical as to what value it would have for a group of remarkable school leaders whose professionalism is outstanding and who are committed to the uplift of the human condition. Eventually, however, I conceded that my rather unusual background, which involved politics and business, as well as studying and lecturing on practical philosophy, would allow something different to be said about surviving and ultimately thriving in school leadership at the highest levels. The current training manuals for newly appointed head teachers focussed more on cultivating their managerial and functional abilities than on leadership in educational institutions whose purpose was to change and improve human lives. Nothing had been written that satisfactorily described the essential view of the head teacher's role or how he or she could best cope with the enormous mental and emotional challenges of the job, day in and day out.

Emotional intelligence is fundamentally the innate knowing of our being. It speaks to us in many different ways, often as an intuition or deep inner certainty, as if it were coming from beyond the mind. It is powerful. It unifies, generating empathy and connectedness. At its best, emotional intelligence allows a sense of Oneness to emerge so life can become cooperative and interdependent, not aggressive and divisive.

The person who can evolve his or her emotional intelligence will benefit significantly from it. With practice, access to this intelligence increases, slowly but steadily. The development of emotional intelligence can result in a conscious decision to live and lead in a certain way. Once someone has tested it and found it to work, a greater belief in oneself emerges, which does not manifest in an egotistical way, but in a quiet inner confidence and humility. Confidence allows the leader to be patient and present to decide what needs to be done. Humility allows the leader to share the burden and not seek the limelight. Together, confidence and humility, both tenets of emotional intelligence, allow for an unshakeable peace at heart and in mind. Emotional intelligence allows the school leader to meet the needs of pupils, teachers, and parents happily, no matter how demanding the situation may be, and it can deliver real personal satisfaction.

The St James Schools, established by my mentor, have from the outset adopted emotional intelligence practices, building them into the core curriculum and the daily programme. We practise Quiet Time and meditation, as well as regular pausing and stopping to allow the mind to fall still and join the present moment. Our ethos is to promote the sense of belonging to the human family, which we call Oneness, and our pedagogy is based on the premise that every child is inherently brilliant. The role of the teacher is to bring out that brilliance. The job of the head teacher is to ignite the divine spark in every pupil and teacher by creating an atmosphere that allows everyone's true nature to flourish. Where that atmosphere is clouded, usually by the sceptics in the corner of the staffroom, the head has to keep working, no matter how much his or her patience is tested, to let each person's brilliance shine forth. There are days when we miss the mark and forget, but with love in our hearts and inspiration in our being, we go back and try again.

This is what emotional intelligence does: it keeps you trying to reach for the best in everyone. It keeps you loving and caring for all the people in your realm, and also trying to reach for the best in yourself, valuing the role you have been given.

His Holiness, the Dalai Lama, recently told an audience I was privileged to be a part of that to evolve a better world, the old ways of thinking about education were no longer adequate. Education must find a way, he told us, to reach the whole of humanity and must be founded on 'warm-heartedness'. Emotional intelligence is the essence of that warmth.

It is natural for people to work with each other for their mutual benefit. Somehow, recent decades have allowed that naturalness to become distorted, and much of education now focusses on pupils learning how to achieve competitive advantages and material gain. These goals, however, are not a satisfactory basis for pedagogy or school leadership because they do not prepare young people to evolve happy, harmonious, and valuable human relations.

The next generation of school leaders and those in the role today, who will forge the new tomorrow, require a different approach. My hope is that this book offers a new and progressive way forward and that it will play a modest part in shaping the future of school leadership.

# Chapter One

# The Reluctant Head

'You must be completely off your trolley!' If those words had been spoken by a close friend, a fully sane man might have listened more carefully, but as they were spoken by me, to myself, moments after being asked to take on the headship of a senior boys school, they were simply ignored. What a fateful decision.

It was my first headship, but more than that, I wasn't even a qualified teacher. In fact, the last time I had been in a head's office was forty years earlier at my own secondary school, an all-boys affair on the North Island of New Zealand. It was vastly different from this small private school in West London with something of a distinctive reputation, owing to the fact that it practises meditation twice a day and had become known as one of the last schools in the UK to abolish caning.

I had last encountered the unmistakable scent of a head's office when my own headmaster, in the midst of elucidating why the school would be better off without me, indicated in no uncertain terms that unless my behaviour improved, the rest of my life would be spent – in a head's office! How prescient. That particular exchange was enough to alter my dream of becoming a teacher (which I'd had since I was twelve) and to take to journalism, which in turn led to work on regional newspapers, local radio, a move to the UK, a spell in the press office of the British Conservative Party, two election campaigns as a press secretary to Margaret Thatcher, the launch of a lobbying business, and a sell-out and lock -out from that sector before I headed back to teaching through a graduate training company and the launch of a charity founded to teach leadership skills to young people. Perhaps teaching was my calling after all. Fate certainly appeared to be saying so. It had only taken thirty-three years to get back to the starting point, a modest amount of time in comparison to the aeons by which history is measured. Life can certainly spring its surprises. Even at fifty-two.

The previous fifty or so years had been good to our family, especially in the material world. We hadn't wanted for much and yet there remained a strange inner dissatisfaction with things. I often heard myself say, in response to questions from friends or colleagues, that I hadn't found my reason or purpose in life yet. 'Well, at your age you should have', one or two retorted, purportedly to be helpful, but only serving to create a slightly darker mood for the next hour or two. Time to open another bottle of Sauvignon.

Too much time was spent on intercontinental flights, some of them related to business and others to lecture tours. I developed a passion for philosophy, and for many years, having realised an inner connection with Eastern meditation, I'd toured the southern hemisphere and the east coast of the United States, lecturing on Platonic thought and Vedantic theory to audiences composed of like-minded men and women, under the auspices of the London-based School of Economic Science. It was certainly time for a change.

St James Senior Boys' School, and its sister and brother schools in London and around the world, emerged in the mid-1970s to meet the challenge posed by the Labour Party, which was threatening the traditional British grammar school. Some of the more vociferous left-wing voices were even threatening to put out of business the traditional English 'public school'. For a New Zealander, it was tricky at first to comprehend how public schools could actually be the most private of all institutions, and why anybody would worry if their demise was hastened. But then I came to understand that such great schools as Eton and Harrow have for generations educated the ruling class, and without them the Empire (or Commonwealth) would probably not have happened. The rampaging socialists in Harold Wilson's government (several of whom later turned out to be non-committal social democrats, but never mind) were hell-bent on destroying generations of educational pedagogy, offering in return a new idea: the comprehensive school. Selection was bad, equality was good – even if it meant the bright could not get brighter and the ladder of escape for talented children from poor areas was being removed.

London barrister Leon MacLaren and the mature students of economics and philosophy under his care at the School of Economic Science wanted an alternative for their own children. MacLaren had a passion for social justice and hated what he was witnessing around him. His own father had been a Labour MP in the Potteries and had fought, unsuccessfully, for years for the rights of the poor. A proper education, he told his students, was the only way out of institutional and social poverty. He inspired them not just to complain about what they saw in front of them, but also to do something about it.

What to do emerged as MacLaren returned again and again from his biannual visits to Varanasi in India, where he would meet with a revered sage of the Shankara tradition, Sri Shantaananda Saraswati. The Shankara tradition propounded a philosophy of Oneness, or unity. Religion might give many names to God, but the spirit of consciousness, truth and bliss lives in the heart of every human being. The approach contained many similarities to the Platonic tradition, which holds that a human being is already full of knowledge and wisdom; he just doesn't realise it. The human purpose in life is to find out about this and to work towards self-knowledge.

In response to MacLaren's questions, the sage unfolded a dynamic educational initiative which teachers today in the midst of their Postgraduate Certificate in Education (PGCE) would find interesting and helpful. Children should be offered the best possible material; the content of lessons should be the best food for the mind. Teachers should give only this finest subject content for the children to absorb, but give it in a way that demonstrated recognition that the children already knew it. This would tease the innate knowledge out of them, as a fly fisherman teases the trout to the water's surface. Teachers should constantly look to keeping themselves and their subjects fresh; if the material is not going down well it should be changed, or the teacher should change his or her approach. A teacher developing a pupil is akin to a potter spinning his wheel: an outer hand of discipline is needed to keep the pot (or child) in shape whilst the inner hand of love continually moves outwards, expanding its creation. Every day should have a balance of activities designed to nourish the spirit, expand the heart, clear the mind and make the body fit. Every child should sing and learn number tables by heart. The great scriptures should be taught and used as core material.

The blend of old and new captivated MacLaren and his students. They asked him if he would start a school for their children; he agreed to provide his help and guidance if they did the work, and for ten years he kept a very close eye on the school's development, making sure that he established an independent board to run the place, which would outlast him and the School of Economic Science. Nearly twenty years after his death, his wisdom is still evident.

When I was working in politics for the British Conservatives in the 1980s, I was also attending MacLaren's philosophy classes. My wife and I had three small children who were approaching school age, and MacLaren's new school appeared the perfect solution to our parental concerns. The founding St James headmaster was an ex-businessman, extremely charismatic in his own idiosyncratic way and the kind of man you would totally trust. The fact that he was a strict disciplinarian – a quality that later landed him in hot water with former students who objected to the caning in his regime – was of tremendous appeal. We knew he was as generous with his love and guidance to our sons as he was firm; the chaos of teenage street gangs and crime in London was not for us, and we certainly wanted something different. So the three boys were put in his care, and from the age of four to eighteen they thrived. Their generosity and mental acuity became a frequent talking point amongst my political friends, many of whom later visited the school or attended its events. For a nondescript school in West London, it was certainly punching above its weight.

Of course, it had its detractors. Anything new, and something not easily understood, often does. Its early years were far from easy, especially the early 1980s when journalists from the *London Evening Standard* sought to brand MacLaren a 'cult leader' because of his Indian connections.

Margaret Thatcher was my boss at the time. The story broke on election day in 1983, with a political twist. It tried to make the case that some senior Liberal candidates were tied to MacLaren's organisations and that he was trying to manipulate them into following his political and 'religious' agenda. The pro-Tory paper and its editor, who was well known to me, had not realised that the Prime Minister's election press secretary was also connected to MacLaren and the School of Economic Science, which has never had a political or religious agenda; it is, in fact, a rather interesting, if somewhat pedantic, philosophical school in the classical Platonic tradition. Despite being on very thin ice, the *Standard* decided to expose my own links to the man and contacted several MPs, hoping to question the re-elected Prime Minister in Parliament about it.

I phoned Downing Street to warn the PM and was told she was in her study having breakfast, a scene I was familiar with, having had breakfasts with her and husband, Denis, while on the election trail. She came to the telephone, listened carefully and then proffered a leadership lesson I would never forget. 'Oh, David, don't worry about me! It's you I'm worried about.' She then set about advising me on how to look after myself, something she often did to her young staff. It is for very good reason that I frequently refer to her as a 'mother figure' in my life, rather than as a boss or mighty political icon.

In fact, we had an interesting relationship over the seven years I was in her employ. Her son, Mark, and I are the same age, and although she loved him deeply, she was clearly frustrated with him. She seemed to view me on many occasions with somewhat 'son-like' status. When I arrived late for a meeting in her study at Downing Street (a frequent occurrence, I confess), she would have kept the seat next to her vacant: as I pushed the study door open, she would command, in her imperious voice, to the latecomer to enter, then pat the chair and say, much to the annoyance of the gathering, 'Oh David, do come and sit here.' They all knew they would have lost their head had they been late, and so a touch of envy arose amongst some colleagues, to say the least. However, she knew that the political lobby of media reporters were prepared to listen to her young spokesman and that, quietly and without the fanfare of the latter-day spin doctors, good stories could be placed by him and rotten ones ameliorated.

She was meritocratic and liked to promote people who she perceived to be efficient and supportive and who would stand up to her, at least to some extent. This came to a head as we were preparing for the 1983 general election campaign. A new invention, Breakfast Television, was just making its way into the national consciousness. I was keen to get away from the daily party-headquarters press conferences ('agenda-setting events'), and to get an early march on other media by 'managing appearances' on the breakfast television programmes.

It was a strategy shared and worked out with Conservative Party Chairman and Cabinet Minister, Cecil Parkinson, and Gordon Reece (later knighted for his political services), as well as other grandees, including advertising mogul Tim Bell (also later ennobled).

We had gathered at the Prime Minister's country residence, Chequers, to present the strategy, but the moment Mrs T raised an objection to the plan ('I am not going to be scheduled or managed by anybody!') the whole lot of them backed off the argument faster than ice cream melts in an inferno. I was left exposed to fight the corner for such a 'revolutionary strategy' (now, common place in every election).

Although young and inexperienced (as Parkinson later graciously described it), I decided to hold my ground. The stubborn colonial lad thought these English toffs surrounding the Prime Minister to be more than a touch sycophantic and gutless. The argument eventually ended: she was the boss, and clearly dismissive of the plans, so the honourable thing to do was to resign. She accepted. But the next day she changed her mind and commanded another of her Rottweilers, the late Sir Ian Gow, her parliamentary private secretary, to get me to change mine. For four months, I didn't, and instead took my P45 tax forms and headed back to journalism. Such stubbornness, cultivated at a tender age, later proved a valuable survival tool in headship.

The story, however, ends nicely, and with another leadership lesson. Stubbornness is less valuable than the virtue of being prepared to give up your pride, especially when the terms before you are the best you are going to get. Mrs T decided to call the election earlier than anticipated when we were at Chequers. The Falklands War had been and gone, successfully and victoriously, the unemployment figures were just starting to fall, and the mood of the country was buoyant. The opposition parties were in disarray and Michael Foot was a brilliant brain in search of friends for his socialist cause; there weren't many. Yet the first week of the campaign was proving far more difficult for the Conservatives to manage than we had expected and the press coverage was appalling.

During Sunday lunch at my in-laws' home, with newspapers scattered everywhere, the phone rang. It was Cecil Parkinson, talking from Central Office campaign headquarters on his speaker phone. 'Mrs T is here with me and we want you to come back. She wants you to run the press side of the campaign, just as you used to. Will you do it?' Of course, it was a tremendous honour, and of course, I was dying to get back into the fray. A touch of haggling over the fee for the job, an agreement that I would resign again on election night no matter what the result, and we were in complete agreement. The scent of the campaign had already filled the air.

'Tell him to meet us tomorrow afternoon in Inverness. Get Central Office to make the travel arrangements', I heard Mrs T tell Cecil from across the room.

It turned out to be an uneventful campaign, delivering a record Conservative Party majority. On election night, Mrs T received my resignation – and Cecil told me that he he'd had a spot of personal difficulty. Ironically, his decision to stay with his charming wife and leave his mistress and her love-child would ultimately lead to his temporary resignation from the Government. That night, however, we both knew that he could not take the role of Foreign Secretary, which he had so wished for. The shame on himself and the Government would be too much if the problem became public, which a few months later it inevitably did. It was not then possible to know how valuable all these experiences would be when later I would have accepted the headship of St James Senior Boys.

Post-election, the plan was to get a proper job and start a business career; teaching children was nowhere on the horizon. A friend had started the first British environmental countryside magazine, a brilliant idea but somewhat ahead of its time. His invitation to become managing editor, a position that would also allow some political journalism, seemed a perfect avenue back to writing and business at the same time. The idea hit the dust when the liquidators moved in a little over a year later and a redundancy notice lay in the in-tray with a request to hand back the company car keys. There was virtually no redundancy pay, and so feeding the children, let alone keeping the eldest at St James, was going to be a challenge.

A political friend advised a look at lobbying. A couple of fledgling businesses were emerging and the 1984 October Conservative Party Conference was about to take place. Attending the event might lead to new contacts and help get something started, he suggested. So down to Brighton I travelled, trying to look busy. Late on Thursday afternoon, the day before the Prime Minister's keynote speech to the political faithful, a group of friends and political journalists gathered in the main bar of the Grand Hotel. There is always quite a buzz on the eve of the leader's speech. However, I had committed to attend a philosophy session with Leon MacLaren that night in London. MacLaren objected to anyone not keeping their given word, but every atom in my political bones was arguing for remaining in Brighton. A friend who was staying at the hotel even offered the spare bed in his twin room. I was completely torn; being so close to the action but out of it is never much fun. Finally I decided: the right thing to do was to go back to London. My philosophy friends then had to suffer hearing about what a tough decision it had been to leave the conference. The next morning, however, it became crystal clear just how fortunate that decision had been.

In the early hours of Friday morning, while Mrs T and the rest of her Cabinet slept soundly in their beds, a bomb planted by the IRA blew up the Grand Hotel in an audacious attempt at political murder and destabilization of our democratic process. Mrs T had miraculously escaped, but some dear political friends and their families had not. I sat in our London home with a sick heart, watching with horror Breakfast TV and the developing story. Providentially, several personal friends had escaped, one of them falling several floors and landing cushioned by his mattress beneath him. Others were trapped in the rubble. What would Mrs T do? What kind of leadership would she now show?

As a leader, she was deeply loyal to her closest staff, another lesson I have tried never to forget. She would be devastated, knowing that Norman Tebbit and his wife, Margaret, were lying somewhere, trapped by tons of fallen masonry. Every fibre in her body would have wanted to scream knowing that Roberta Wakeham, wife of her Chief Whip, was dead along with other leading party figures including Sir Anthony Berry. Five years earlier, in 1979, on the eve of her first election victory, she had lost her close confidant, Airey Neave, in a car bombing in the underground car park of the House of Commons – and now this. Somehow, in a crisis, the leader has to dig deep and find inner sources of energy not previously known, just to carry on when every bone in the body is screaming not to.

'The conference will carry on', she declared. 'Terrorism will not defeat the democratic process!' The party faithful, who had been standing in the Brighton streets dressed in pyjamas and dressing gowns, found their way to a Marks & Spencer shop and replaced something of their wardrobes, at least enough to let them appear at the conference opening that morning at 9.30 a.m., according to schedule. Commentators later described it as one of Mrs Thatcher's finest Churchillian moments. Even her political enemies, of whom there were many, had to admire her. Crises usually define a leader. In this case, it not only gave Britain's first woman prime minister enormous fresh credibility, but it also set a modern standard for crisis management globally.

The headship at St James Senior Boys did not, at first, appear to be a position involving crisis-management. Of course, the unexpected was expected, but surely this would be a fine opportunity to implement some deeper thoughts on what education should be. This depth seemed lacking in the modern British educational system, and although the world could not be changed, a start might be made.

I had spent the seven previous years running a training and personal development consultancy company, working with some of the brightest young graduates in several of Europe's leading manufacturing and consumer companies. That had come about after the sale of my lobbying company to an American marketing polymath that wanted access to European politicians in Brussels and Bonn, as well as Paris and London. The sale of the European Political Lobbying Group, which had evolved over ten years, had locked me out of the 'profession' for several years, and so it was time to try something new.

Working with graduates, one thing became clear. Academic achievements are only a part of what makes good managers and are even less relevant to what will make them become great leaders. Leaders need vision. Working so closely with Mrs T had shown that. Leaders need to know how to speak that vision into existence; how to carry people with them in the face of opposition; how to keep going when nearly everyone appears to be against you. She had taught all these things too. The young graduates were found to have very few of the personal skills needed to accomplish much of anything. Their strategy formulation was fine, but getting that strategy to work required a whole different set of skills that they did not have, and which schools, in my view, needed to teach, because universities clearly were not doing so.

When I accepted the headship, I hoped the position might allow an evolution of philosophical understanding amongst the young. The world of religion was becoming divisive, with the rise of Islamic fundamentalists and a none-too-pleasant response by fundamentalists of other faiths, including certain elements of Christianity. The scientific community, with its purely empirical vision of life, was creating a one-dimensional physical view of human existence, totally ignoring the brilliance and creative intelligence inherent in the whole of nature. It appeared an apposite moment to start to formulate a new vision of human potential – a new way for youngsters to tap in to their own creativity, their own magnificence, their own spirituality. We needed a spiritual response, not a religious or material one, to the challenges of the world around us.

Taking on a headship to become a paper-pushing administrator seemed a waste of time. To make any difference at all, there would have to be opportunities to teach and offer what was possible based on the philosophy and view of life that I had studied and experienced over the previous thirty years. The ideal would be to teach every boy. However, to achieve this, a significant handicap had to be overcome, which most prospective heads would not have to face. I had never taught in a formal educational setting before and had certainly never taught boys' classes. Being a father of three sons only partly prepares you for standing in front of twenty testosterone-driven fifteen-year-olds, talking about the love of wisdom.

For the first term I awoke every morning feeling wretched . How do you take an assembly? What do you say? How do you stop them misbehaving? How do you guide a teacher in a subject you have no knowledge of? How do you capture the attention of a class?

What is a lesson objective? How do you suspend a boy? The day-to-day stuff of running a school, which experience as a classroom teacher or deputy head would help prepare one for, was simply absent. I was at sea and the threat of drowning was high.

The staffroom was sharply divided with regard to their new headmaster. Several senior members who wanted the job had been overlooked by the governors, and everyone wondered what life would be like having a novice in education with a businessman's reputation at the helm. The governors had decided that no internal candidate could win the support of the rest of the staff, and as none had received any leadership or management training, they were unlikely to be able to bring about the change that was needed. That is not to say they weren't short of opinions on what was needed and how it should happen. Some made it very plain they fully resented the new appointment, and this made me feel even worse.

The outgoing headmaster, though unwell, had met me on several occasions to discuss in general terms the particular nature of a St James education, seeking to ensure a continuing connection with the founder's principles. That was very helpful, but as to guidance on the day-to-day running of the institution, he was not so keen to tell. For him, with retirement looming, control and command of a school had become second nature, and for anybody to transmit what is embedded in them as their nature is curiously not very easy. Eventually, our meetings stopped.

When I arrived the first morning at the new job, feeling even more anxious than usual, it was clear that the new office must be one of the nicest of any headmaster in London. Its view overlooking the River Thames and its beautiful sun-filled balcony combined to create an atmosphere of deep tranquillity. That tranquillity would turn out to be a lifesaver on many subsequent occasions, but on that dreadful morning, the sight of the river passed me by. All I could see was a wave of blue-jacketed boys streaming through the door, several of them for the first time. There was no written plan as to what to do with them all, and no clear directions as to where the new boys should go.

My eyes fell on an envelope on the head's desk, which I was to inherit. My name was on it. 'Oh, how wonderful!' I thought. 'A good-luck message from a well-wisher. How thoughtful!' I opened it and looked down. It was a bill, left over from the summer holidays. Something in me still managed a laugh.

Eventually, the whole school gathered for assembly in our meeting hall. Every pair of eyes was on the new man. I had only been to one full assembly at the school and had never tried to take one. I reached out to the deputy, a wonderful man who from that first day until now has shown nothing but support and loyalty. 'What the hell do I do?' I asked him. He took a piece of paper and wrote down a list: 'Get them quiet. Dedicate the day to the Supreme Lord. Say the Lord's Prayer and other prayers if you like. Speak a psalm with them, antiphonally. Give a very short homily. Get them singing. Get out!' I could barely wait for the last item on the list.

During one of my interviews for the job, a governor who had been involved in founding the school asked me how I would cope with coming to the same place and doing the same sort of thing day after day. He didn't warn me about the drama of assemblies or teaching classes or suspending boys or coping with super-demanding parents. He clearly didn't know the detail of the kind of day a headmaster faces: staff meetings, new parent meetings, investigations into disciplinary issues, formulating budgets, grappling with child-protection and with health and safety legislation, answering complaints, counselling bereaved pupils, discussing curriculum and assessment ... and the list goes on. I may have had some interesting jobs before, but none of them had the variety and spice of this one.

In addition, if this job was going to be fulfilling in the long run, it needed to satisfy my inner aspirations – what in leadership terms we call *intent*. What is the point in being a manager? Teaching is, after all, a vocation, a calling. To open the minds and hearts of young people to the limitless possibilities of their incarnations is worth the pain and the effort – but to push acres of paper around a fancy desk isn't. I decided to teach every boy every week, on a forty per cent timetable. 'Crazy!' the inspectors later said. 'Not so', was my reply then. And so it continues to this day.

Several years on, it has become clear that taking a headship requires a passion. Not a passion for the trappings of leadership, but a passion to want to do your very best to change the state of the minds and hearts of young people. I wonder why so many head teachers no longer teach. The traditional route to the top in school leadership is through the classroom, so why leave it completely when the top job beckons? The common view is that it is not possible to manage the paper work and teach meaningfully at the same time. I understand that, especially as the regulatory mountain has grown exponentially these last few years, with well over 180 regulations to tick in the box, a threefold increase over the past half-decade. But it is possible. It requires extremely good deputies and younger colleagues willing to take on responsibility. It requires working very long days and most weekends. It requires an ability to prioritise – pupils first, paper later. But it can be done.

Even after years of experience, there is so much still to learn in running a school, but I have discovered this: good education comes from the heart – your own heart and the hearts of your pupils and their teachers. In a spiritual context, you have to love them, limitlessly, for who they are; to see that they are already brilliant human beings. You have to work tirelessly with your colleagues so they see how much their brilliance can be brought forth. This is the essential meaning of the Latin *educare*, 'to lead out', or educate.

Headship is a proper job. I have never felt more challenged, even when working for Mrs Thatcher. Equally, I have never enjoyed anything more, even with the pain and frustration that inevitably comes with the territory, because headship is creating futures and shaping humanity. It is helping to build communities of values-based citizens who acknowledge their own freedoms and, at the same time, their responsibilities towards others. I know of no other role in life that can do that so effectively and with such a long-lasting effect.

# Chapter 2

# Being You

A GREAT THING ABOUT A fourteen-year-old boy in an assembly hall is that he is always ready and willing and often exceptionally able to slice you open at the drop of a hat. In fact, he may wait for just the right moment to do it. He may even be prepared to store up evidence over time to make his lunge more effective when the moment comes.

Some of these bandits have learnt their trade from their parents, who make an art form of trying to expose the head's weaknesses or catch his inconsistencies and throw them back at him. Sometimes, they are in cahoots with those staffroom cronies who complain that their teaching programme is so heavy that they have only a spare hour or two a day to while away their time plotting your downfall. Fortunately, the vast majority of staff and parents are not like that at all. However, if you want spirited pupils you will find it beneficial to keep encouraging the bandits to make their slingshots even more sophisticated. Headship is on central stage, all day and every day. The only hope of survival is to be you!

The best heads I have met since joining their ranks have certainly been characters, but not particular types of character. Some are noisy and boisterous; others are quiet. Some wear their personalities on their sleeve for all to see; others just quietly get on with the job. Some are bulls and some are butterflies. It is not the personality that makes them brilliant at the job. It is the fact that they know who they are and that they are confident in their own skin. Experience helps, but it is the self-knowledge and the confidence that goes with it that makes the real difference.

Knowing yourself is the first factor in all forms of leadership, and it is critical in headship. The trouble is, who you think you are is often not who others think you are, and so conflict can arise. Therefore, cultivating some inner tools for self-reflection is a very beneficial beginning.

As this book is an emotional intelligence guide, I am not going to discuss the dubious value of 'outer tools', such as 360-degree feedback and independent appraisal, so beloved of management gurus. The place to start is with yourself because you are with yourself every waking hour of the day.

Most of us think we are what our bodies, thoughts, and feelings tell us. If your gut hurts, you think, 'I am hurting'. If you are insulted by someone, you think, 'I am insulted'. If we think of a brilliant idea, we tend to claim it. If we don't quite get the point, we are often prepared to blame someone else's poor communication. Nearly all our self-perceptions are centred on our bodies, thoughts, and feelings. And yet there is a fourth dimension which is available to us all but which we so often ignore: the conscious intelligence that knows all of this.

When the psalmist told us, 'Be still and know that I am God', he wasn't just highlighting the impact and importance of what is known when we become still. He was telling us that there is an inner Knower who watches and waits and simply observes everything that is happening in our bodies, minds, and emotions. This Knower turns out to be the real 'I' referred to in the scriptures of nearly all the great religions and philosophies. But this 'I' becomes identified with the body and its functions, and with the mind and its thoughts and feelings. It is this identification that causes pain and suffering, not whatever is happening.

An insult is nothing but that. Let it pass and it will drift away like driftwood in a river. A failure will pass and so will a peel of praise, just so long as you let it. But the mind grasps and holds and says, 'This is me.' No, it is not! You are the Knower watching it. The rest is stuff that is passing, but you, the ever-present, conscious witnessing self, are not. You are the unmoving.

This is probably one of the toughest leadership lessons of headship: not to identify with the things that are happening to you and through you. I am not advising that you don't pay heed to or take responsibility for what is taking place in your mind and emotions. My suggestion is that you come to know yourself as the witness of it, because by doing so you will gain stability and a clearer insight into what is happening to both yourself and the people around you.

Every human being is a four-dimensional person. In the West, we only usually recognize three parts: the body, mind, and heart. The fourth part, always acknowledged in the East, is the power of conscious awareness, which is intrinsically available to everyone. The equation is simple: Know yourself as the power of conscious awareness, and the stings and arrows that land in the heart and mind can be more clearly deciphered and let go. If a head teacher can come to know this, the pains of the job will still be felt, but they will not linger. He or she will start to see things more objectively; therefore, he will see more. By seeing more he will know better what is to be done.

The analogy of the mountain climber is a good one. At base camp, the mountain looks huge and possibly insurmountable. But as he climbs step by step up the mountainside, gaining a clearer perspective of his path to the top and the surrounding plains, that which seemed so daunting at first now appears manageable. Climbing the inner mountain of awareness has much the same effect. As you step higher up the awareness ladder, the issues at ground level become easier to deal with.

Getting to know who you are requires work. We must cultivate our inner power of awareness (see chapter 3). The first thing that comes into view when we start cultivating this conscious power within us is the murky world of mixed emotions. We want to do a good job and make the right decisions, but what if we get it wrong?

Thoughts can creep in, such as, 'The last time I did this I made a complete mess, but I can't remember just what went wrong'. Such thoughts, which bring the sense of inadequacy and doubt, can paralyse the head, who needs to take many decisions, often very quickly.

What we need to realise is that the murkiness is usually because we think our real self is in the middle of the situation, whereas our real self is unencumbered by our emotional lack of clarity; hence, the need to stop and step back from the confusion. The secret is to climb the awareness ladder. As we climb up, the atmosphere becomes more rarefied, and as we become more still, centred, and attentive, we can let the sediment and agitation settle. Then we can see what has to be done. The key to gaining this clarity is not in doing something – it is in *stopping* doing for a little while. It is to pause.

The sages of old had a great leadership tip. 'Practice patience', they said, 'because with patience comes confidence'. Watching patiently as you climb the awareness ladder and your emotions settle is far easier to describe than to do, but with practice it becomes entirely possible. You will not read in many popular magazine articles on leadership about the 'patient' leader; in fact, the chap who describes sorting everything out in days and months usually gets the plaudits. But something that a head can apply over time, and that serves in a variety of situations, is needed.

I found on assuming headship that awareness and patience had to be the first of several virtues practised. In the interval between my appointment and the beginning of the school year, it proved possible to interview every member of staff and about two-thirds of the pupils. I wanted to find out what made each of them tick, so we went through what I called an 'emotional contract conversation'. I simply asked them to illuminate the way they liked to work, how they felt about different things in life and school, what they paid attention to, and what was important to them in forming working or social relationships. I kept notes of each conversation, and several years on still referred to them when considering internal staff appointments. At the very least, it helped to shape various jobs to fit the people on offer to do them.

Very quickly, a checklist of things to do mounted up, and with every conversation the list seemed to get longer. Quite plainly, some prioritisation was needed. In addition, money was required to tackle the projects. That part was simple: the governors informed me that there was none. If radical change was to take place, it would have to happen without the sweetener of redundancy payments or, at the other end, golden hellos. Welcome to the world of school leadership! Goodbye, business practices.

There are in fact very few days in the school year when change can actually take place – when you can communicate a message that resonates and leads to new ways of doing things. I counted only seven days in the year: the days of our staff in-service training meetings. Trying to make changes while the train was heading full steam along the track of the academic year was virtually impossible. Patience it had to be! This proved a godsend.

The more the patience, the clearer it became as to who could do what and by when. Some characters in the staffroom began to show talents and interests I had not previously spotted; others raised their hands for jobs they hadn't done before.

The chattering classes also took advantage of patience required for the unfolding of the plan. 'He said he would bring change and he is doing nothing', said one vociferous staffer. 'He doesn't understand us and what we have to put up with', was another refrain. There was sympathy, too. Overall, I had a growing confidence that there would be a right time to act and that when it arrived, the knowledge of what to do would be clear. Awareness is an extraordinarily practical tool.

Awareness also allows you to see the ideas that shape the mind and in turn transform into action. It usually happens surprisingly quickly, often sparked by just a single word or thought – and like a bullet once fired, it can't be retrieved.

Thoughts, however, can be seen as they unfold, although it takes a real effort to cultivate mental awareness. The power that the ability to see thoughts gives the leader is remarkable. It stops mistakes but, more importantly, it propels good ideas and sows those seeds everywhere.

Often the leader has a desire to do something but before he knows it, a doubt has arisen. Doubt is frequently the bed partner of desire. If we are not watching carefully, the mind quickly turns into the idea, 'I am not certain about this', and the action changes shape or stops altogether. Another impulse or resolve to carry on may arise, but it too may be quickly overshadowed by worry or fear. Fear is a significant enemy of the leader because it freezes action. The only way out of fear is to see it for what it is by climbing the awareness ladder, by being patient and certain that the knowledge of what to do will come when it is needed, and by having the confidence to follow it when it does so.

When inexperienced leaders start to spot this sequence of mental movement, they realise that a huge element of what they might call 'faith' is involved in making things happen. But it is not faith in another that is required; it is faith in oneself. And that can only be firm when you know yourself.

During the whole of my first year, the swing of personal, emotional, and mental movement was, perhaps understandably, quite vigorous. Discipline in the school was poor and there was no standardised system of punishment or reward. Boys were taking subjects they were unsuited for. Registration systems were haphazard. Most staff members wanted to do something about these things, but what to do was not easy for everyone to agree on. We had to wait until we could see the problems more clearly and then act. When we finally did so, the clarity of decisions was encouraging. A red and yellow card system, like the one used on the football pitch, came into play to help discipline; a system of rewards emerged which all teachers adopted and applied. A new curriculum was planned, and heads of department, who had been in low-key roles until this point, started to exercise their considerable professional expertise. The policy of patience was paying dividends, and as I gained confidence that what we were doing was right, so too did more of the staff. Their perceptions of what was happening began to change, albeit rather slowly in some cases.

The Buddha tells us we are shaped by our perceptions and that most of those perceptions are related to what is happening to our bodies and to changes in our minds and emotions. If I am anxious and nervous, and if I fail to be aware that the feelings are passing, then I will start to see anxiety everywhere. My projected world will be coloured by doubt and nervousness. But if I grasp that my perceptions are loaded by my thoughts and feelings, and that they need to be examined very carefully before I take them to be real, I can step back and feel relieved of the push and pull of the events I am meeting.

Stepping back gives us an opportunity to practice another leadership virtue too: forgiveness. Forgiveness is not some holy operation involving direct intervention of the Divine. It is a practical tool to turn things around. To forgive is to give something better or something finer than you have received. It is easy in headship to embrace the perception that people are against you when the reality is that you may not be communicating your ideas as well as you could or that someone disagrees with only one of your points. Disagreement does not mean someone dislikes you. One long-serving staff member was invited to join the senior leadership team after he gave up a campaign of headmaster-resistance. 'I used to think you were the devil', he once told me, 'but now I don't think that. I think I can see what you are trying to do'. He is an excellent teacher and wise educationalist, and it is far better for us all that he is onside, rather than offside throwing bricks. In regular conversations with him, I would always try to mention one of his praiseworthy qualities, even if we disagreed on some points. Eventually, unbeknown to me, he started to do the same. The result of giving something finer back to each other was that we ultimately forgave each other, and what emerged was a new respect on both sides.

The tool of forgiveness is also very useful when it comes to holding your ground in an argument, something new heads need to do frequently. When staff members get frustrated because you are not responding positively or in the way they want, they are likely to accuse you of 'not listening'. First, you have to check inwardly that this is not the case; then, assuming it is not the case, you can gently inform them that you *are* listening – you just are not agreeing with everything they say. Spell it out, in writing if it helps, and then try to find something to agree with, or simply to go along with, so you are giving something finer back. This requires watchfulness and awareness of one's inner world at all times.

One staff member became very frustrated because she felt she was not being heard and the troubles of her department were not being attended to. She had something of a point but she used the cruise missile form of middle management communication to get my attention. She hoped the bombs she was lobbing in my direction would cause enough damage to force a change. The best approach was to confront her directly and ask why she thought I was both doing what I was, and, more importantly, not doing other things she wanted done. The second part of the question stumped her.

'So are you telling me that it is a conscious decision of yours *not* to do these things I am asking for?' she finally asked.

'Yes.'

'Why are you *not* doing what I am asking for?'

'Great! That's a good question. Now we can start talking properly and listen to each other', I replied, before explaining how a conscious decision, not a neglectful one, had been informing the action. She still didn't like the decision, but at least she became quiet and listened attentively. Even better, I started to listen to her too. What had been a terrible relationship became workable. That was a start.

The physical demands of headship are immense. The days are long, and for most of us, term time is relentless. We have to try to stay fit in all the worlds (see chapter 11); it is essential to be aware of when your body is exhausted and what it is telling you.

One tip from the world of business is never to take an important decision when the body is extremely tired. If your body is saying it needs more sleep, the Knower is speaking. Listen to it. The remarkable thing is that the vast majority of decisions *can* wait, and that when you do wait until you are fresh again, the decision is much better. (The time to watch in particular is Friday afternoon.) Perceptions fogged over by tiredness never lead to good decision-making.

Some new heads, freshly into the position, look around for a role model and try in their first year or two to mirror the model's past and present speech and actions. Too often they fail and become disheartened in the process. The reason is simple: the model is not them! Of course, a person's actions can be studied to determine why he or she did things and, in some cases, how those things were done. But copies are never as valuable as originals, and never so effective either. Role models can stimulate reflection, but the leader has to find out who he is for himself, and be that.

The Oracle at Delphi famously declared the first step in eternal wisdom: *Know yourself.* Taking that knowledge into the world requires that we *be* ourselves. There are things to learn and styles to adopt (see chapter 7), but the successful head will always be true to himself or herself. We all swing the golf clubs a little differently, because we have different physical bodies, mental ideas, and emotional content. What we all have in common, however, is the power of conscious awareness. This is the power that lets everything that is happening be observed and not identified with. Harnessing that power is perhaps the greatest challenge of all.

## Exercises for Personal Growth in Awareness

There are countless exercises that will help you grow in awareness, but the simplest are the best. The real key is to practise something every day, even for a short period.

### Conscious Breathing while Counting

1. Become aware of the inward breath as it enters the nostrils.
2. Breathe out, with the attention focussed on an area approximately two inches below the navel.
3. On the inward breath, count the number *one*.
4. On the outward breath, count *two*.
5. On the next inward breath, count *three*.
6. On the next outward breath, count *four*.
7. Try to get to ten without losing attention or focus.

If your attention wanders (everybody's does at some point), just start again.

When you have done this ten times without losing focus, amend the exercise.

1. Count *one* on the inward breath; count *one* on the outward breath.
2. Then count *two* on the inward breath; count *two* on the next outward breath.
3. And so on. Once again, try and get to ten without losing focus.

If you can manage this ten times, you will have increased your power of awareness enormously.

### A Walking Meditation

For so much of the time, we do things mechanically. The most mechanical actions are the ones we do all the time, such as walking, talking, sitting, and eating.

When walking in the school playground, with eyes and ears wide open, try a simple walking meditation. Walk very slowly, aware of each breath, and with each breath, speak to yourself thus:

| | |
|---|---|
| *On the inward breath* | **I have arrived.** |
| *On the outward breath* | **I am home.** |
| *On the inward breath* | **In the here.** |
| *On the outward breath* | **In the now.** |
| *On the inward breath* | **I am fluid.** |
| *On the outward breath* | **I am free.** |
| *On the inward breath* | **In the eternal.** |
| *On the outward breath* | **I abide.** |

With gratitude to Zen Master Thich Nhat Hahn for the foundation of this exercise.

### Watching the Movements of the Mind

The cultivation of this particular ability enables one of the greatest senses of freedom to arise that you will ever experience. Just as the clouds in the sky can be watched without anxiety, by letting them pass, so too can the ideas in the mind be watched and, importantly, allowed to pass.

That which watches I call 'the Knower'. The wise sages of old called it the Witness or Independent Observer. It is that which knows whatever is going on.

1. Close your door for a few minutes. Be on your own.
2. Sit as comfortably as you can, but keep both feet on the floor and your back straight. Be at ease. Begin by becoming aware of any tension in the body and just allowing it to pass. The key is *allowing,* so do not hurry this step.
3. Close the eyes. Become immediately aware of the great space that exists behind the eyes. You, the Knower, are now watching that space. The world of colour and form has momentarily dissolved, but you remain, just watching.

4. Watch the thoughts and ideas that arise. Stay there as the Knower. Let the thoughts come; let them pass. Do not try to grab hold of any one of them. Try to stay focussed on the unmoving space behind them. Do not worry if thoughts don't come; that is fine too.

5. When the attention gets diverted (and one of the ideas gets you), just let the idea go and come back to the watching and the inner space.

6. Try to practise this for five minutes. There is no success or failure, so be neutral and avoid self-criticism.

This simple exercise teaches so much. At the beginning, we may feel frustrated. We may wonder why we can't keep our attention centred on the space. We start to see the pulling power of ideas and how quickly we become identified with them. Just let go and try again. With regular practice, you will gain an enormous power to be aware of what is going on around you and within you. You will also find a new level of inner energy (see chapter 11).

## Staff Inset Exercise

### *Emotional Contract Conversations – Who Am I?*

Pair up members of your Senior Management Team (SMT), preferably putting people together who do not know each other so well. Estimate about an hour and a half for the first part of this exercise.

1. One partner begins by exploring how the other likes to work. He or she asks questions to discover what kind of working habits and patterns bring out the best in his partner: Are you methodical? Do you keep lists? What kind of work gives you the buzz and what drives you mad? The purpose is to increase self-awareness regarding how the person likes to work best.

2. The same partner then asks about the *feelings* the other has about the work he or she does and the way he does it. What

situations or kinds of work create positive feelings? What creates negative feelings? The emphasis is on feelings.

3.  The same partner then asks about *attention*. What does the other like to give the most attention to? Is it detail? Is it broad-brush? Is it planning? Is it assessment? The key is to try to illuminate for the speaker what he or she is naturally drawn to, and what he may prefer to leave aside, giving it less attention.

4.  The same partner finally asks about *relationships* at work. How does the person like to be treated at work? How important are working relationships and in what ways does he like to develop and nurture them? The key is to try to get the speaker to see how he likes to work with colleagues and what brings out the best in him or her.

5.  Once all four topics have been covered (taking about thirty to forty minutes altogether), everyone swops roles and repeats the process.

Note: The questioner should not comment while his or her partner is answering. The answers are not so much for the questioner as for the speaker – so he or she may heighten his own self-awareness.

In the second part of the emotional contract exercise, all the members of the SMT come together. They tell the rest of the team what they have discovered about their partners and what they have found about themselves. This can take several hours. My advice is not to hurry. As the exercise goes on, the participants will find themselves naturally becoming more deeply reflective. A reflective leadership team is excellent. (Make sure you take regular breaks and provide tea, coffee, and sustenance during the feedback session.)

The whole exercise should be repeated every few years, or when the SMT/SLT (Senior Leadership Team) experiences a major change.

# Chapter 3

# Who's There?

A CRUSTY OLD POLITICAL HAND once gave a tip on how to ensure that you get your way at a meeting: make sure you have control of the minutes. The rationale is simple. Every person at the meeting is seeing, hearing, feeling, and thinking about things differently, so make sure yours is the primary record of events.

Whereas Machiavelli may have been proud of his argument, the important point is that the minds and emotions of the people you are leading and working with are impermanent – and yours are too. You may think everyone is on the same page, but chances are they are not. Even if someone's ideas appear similar to your own, his or her page will be tinged and laced with his own perceptions, thoughts, and feelings. That is just the way we as human beings are. And those perceptions, thoughts, and feelings will change constantly, depending on the energy in the room, the inner state each person is experiencing, and the various tendencies each of us has built up over a long period of time. This is the culmination of what we call 'experience'; and we identify with it and call it 'me'. Again, this is human nature.

Realising that all experience is impermanent provides a liberating perspective which, when fully understood, can be harnessed to great effect. It means that the most suspect of characters in the staffroom, or the most recalcitrant head of a department, is capable of change, especially if you know how to reach into someone's inner recesses. The very idea 'he will never change' is a negative and debilitating one, for yourself and for the other person.

So who really is the person we have to lead and deal with, day in day out? As was mentioned in the previous chapter, the Oracle at Delphi gave the first instruction: *know yourself.* Now, flip that coin over and read the second direction: know the person in front of you as not essentially different from you. This is despite appearances, perhaps even significant ones, which at first will appear to contradict this advice.

When Jesus gave the great commandment, 'Love thy neighbour as thyself', he was really saying the same thing. Quite naturally, in seeking to honour this direction, we have usually concentrated on caring for the neighbour but missed the notion that he is to be cared for as myself, whereas in all essential ways, that is who he turns out to be.

Something rather magical happens when you practice seeing the other person as no one other than yourself. Even the most recalcitrant bull in the china shop loses some of his aggression, maybe not immediately, but after not too much effort on your part. Instead of an 'eye for an eye' making, as Gandhi put it, 'the whole world blind', the seeds of Oneness and unity are sown. At a baseline level this approach builds respect. At a deeper level it builds tolerance and understanding, willingness and trust. These qualities must be developed if anybody is to follow you.

When the person in front of you is seen as just like you, another curious ability arises: a kind of inner knowing or intuition. You start to see what that person needs and you can begin to put before him or her the kind of opportunities that he will thrive on and which will help him grow – because you would like to grow too! In the language of self-awareness (introduced in chapter 2) the Knower, you, becomes expansive and aware of the very qualities in the person in front of you that you share. Division and aggression, the stuff of old-style leadership, disappears and a new form of emotional intelligence becomes practical and available.

Your moods are better managed in all human interactions because you know, inwardly, you are dealing with someone who shares your own human essence. A natural empathy arises, not a false accommodation of another's ideas or foibles. A far greater awareness is present in conversation. The listening is finer; the comprehension better. You are not trying to score points and, importantly, you are giving plenty of space for everyone to grow. It is the lack of subtle space that stifles good conversation and, along with it, human development.

In the West we are deeply conscious of our individuality and personality. It has become an all-important god that must be nurtured and protected at all times. The Eastern perspective is different. The ego-self, when expanded, is seen as the very impediment to human interaction and to growth. Self-discovery – uncovering the conscious awareness that is permanent as distinct from everything that is impermanent – is the real direction that is encouraged, whilst at the same time a vision of Oneness is cultivated. The sense of Oneness is everywhere, if we know how to look for it.

Fundamentally, the form of the person in front of us is constituted of the same elements as those in our own form. The earth, water, fire, air, and ether, which even the scientific community agree constitute all bodies, are identical in all of us. When our corpses are put in boxes at the end of life, the elemental bodies break down into the same constituent parts and make the same quantity of ash. So much for individuality here!

We are proud of our particular mental abilities. But really, how different are our thoughts? We mostly accept the same premises of social life, because this is part of the human condition and part of where and how we live together. We think about procreation, provision, protection, growth, and decay. We think about what we have and what we don't have. We fret if we can't get something and worry that what we have might be taken away one day. We are proud of our achievements, but when looked at in detail, those glories are often the product of a series of forces coming together. Not one of us is truly independent – we just think we are.

Our feelings are also not much different from each other's. We all want to love and be loved. We all feel fear and despair, even if the causes are different. Most of us suffer at some time in our lives and seek ways of relieving that suffering. Some meditate, others exercise, some study, and still others might visit the local betting shop, but we are all seeking ways to be happy. Recognition of the pursuit of human happiness is a considerable force in appreciating human Oneness.

Finally, there is the power of awareness itself, with which every human being has the ability to cognise, recognize, and know. Usually, in dealing with each other, we focus on the different things that we see or understand, rather than accepting that the very power of seeing and understanding – the power of intuition, the power of the Knower – is the same in all of us. To accept this is to come to see that a pure intelligence is running through every person, and that intelligence is the same in us all.

Simple reasoning can help lead us to the vision that we are in essence very much like each other. To see the person in front of you as no different from you is not just a fanciful notion of the emotional intelligence gurus. It has substance in reality and is a practical tool in leadership.

The practice is to focus first on the essence of the person before you, not on the superficial differences. The practice is to let the emotion of Oneness prevail and work with the apparent differences so that they do not become a separating force. Separation only ever leads to mistrust and division.

The paradox, when learning how to lead from this vision of Oneness, is that the unity of human essence does not mean each person needs or requires the same things, nor does it mean that each person can be led, or can lead, in the same way. If that were so, we would be living in a world of bland monotony. The world is not like that.

The differences between us are just in our perception, in the shape of our thinking and the quality of our feelings. If we take the perceptions, thoughts, and feelings of the other person to be all that he or she is, we will miss the real person that is there. We will be left with something impermanent, something that is certain to alter, and we will be confused when that person suddenly changes his mind or feels differently, particularly about what we as leaders are trying to do.

As leaders, we are comforted when those who follow us share our perceptions, thoughts, and feelings, but if they don't, it does not mean they are against us, nor are they our enemies. If we think in this negative way when they don't see eye to eye with us, they will become against us. We will consolidate our own opposition. But if we know that in reality we all have the same essence, we can embrace different opinions, different ideas, and different ways of seeing things. Then we can decide which are acceptable or useful and which are not, and move on in the spirit of Oneness.

Intuition and, above all, trust in it help us sort out this leadership paradox: 'The person I am leading is in essence not different from me. He perceives, thinks, and feels with the same power of consciousness as I do, and yet sees things, feels them, and thinks about them somewhat differently'. The key is to harness the differences – from the perspective of Oneness.

Nelson Mandela achieved this brilliantly in the development of South Africa. Having emerged after twenty-seven years on Robben Island, where he was incarcerated by white men with totally different patterns of perception, thought, and feeling, he reached into himself and declared that the new South Africa, including white, coloured, and black people, would be one nation. It would be a rainbow state, embracing all the differences within the single notion of unity. All the things that so easily divide peoples and nations were addressed and given respect and a sense of equality. There would not be one official language – all eleven languages would be classified official. And right from the beginning of his tenure he put out a sound: 'May all be happy. May all be without disease. May all creatures have well-being and none be in misery of any sort'. This ancient prayer, drawn from the Vedantic tradition in India, was used by Mandela at his inauguration. He wanted unity. He wanted

Oneness. And he knew that the things in our humanity which we share and which unite us are far more important than the ephemeral perceptions, thoughts, and feelings that divide us.

Putting out the sound of Oneness in leadership is an approach to modern leadership that is beginning to catch on. The work on emotional intelligence, led so brilliantly by Daniel Goleman (*Emotional Intelligence*) is based on the building of empathy through accessing an intelligence that resides in the emotional centre of everyone. What Goleman and his colleagues have succeeded in showing is that those leaders who manage to grow this power of emotional intelligence are more successful than those who don't, because they become capable of utilising it with everyone they lead. When that intelligence flows freely within an organisation, there is a natural rise in the level of happiness and well-being because people are set free to be brilliant. There is a natural willingness to follow such leaders. The happy ship is one that navigates successfully.

---

Achieving well-being and happiness in a school is no easy matter. Daily I find it a challenge, and some days are better than others.

Having interviewed nearly every member of staff and most of the pupils before starting the job, I had a clear idea of their 'emotional contract': what made them tick. The conversations had also brought to the surface school tensions, which were based on perceptions, thoughts, and feelings. There were plenty.

A clutch of old hands had a grudging admiration for each other, but it was the grudges that often appeared on the sleeve, not the admiration. Some of them had wanted the headship and been passed over. All of them had not wanted any of the others to get the headship; so at least the new circumstances made them all happy in that regard. What intuition clearly highlighted was that they had felt repressed: they wanted to say more and, in some cases, to do more for the welfare of the school. This needed to be embraced.

A gaggle of younger hands, some of them old boys of the school who had returned to teach, had a sweep of fresh ideas and were frustrated by the elders. They wanted to tuck the old guard away in a cupboard and introduce new methods, some of which would cause thrombosis to the traditionalists. The possibility of division leading to unbridgeable chasms was great indeed.

I find in experience that sorting out such issues is not so much a matter of endlessly thinking through the possibilities; it is more a matter of trying to empty the mind, rest in stillness, place the attention on the problem single pointedly, and trust the intuition, which inevitably arises. In this case, the knowledge that emerged from this reflection was to establish, in the beginning, two groups – one for the older hands called the Heads Advisory Group (HAG) and one for the younger ones called the Senior Management Team (SMT). The remit of the HAG was to advise on policy and strategic direction – which they did brilliantly. The role of the SMT was to run the school on a daily basis. They needed to show the older hands they could do it, and within months they had the place singing as it had not done before. They were brilliant. (See chapter 6.)

It was clear that this arrangement could not be a final one and it was clear that the sense of Oneness was not complete. It was, however, a step towards it. Time would have to play its part, as it so often does.

Key players needed to be placed. The level of professional development had been minimal to date and several of the characters were woefully undertrained to do the jobs being asked of them. Their hearts were committed, however, and we began to see early shoots of co-operation and, importantly, understanding emerging between the two groups. Intuition again appeared and I decided to announce that the placement of key individuals in key roles was a temporary matter; there would be a review after two years. Each person accepted the fact that they were, in effect, on a two-year trial for the role they had been asked to perform. The practice of patience would be needed again.

Two years on, the awareness of who was playing to what strengths was obvious to everyone, and it became a far simpler matter to move the players around. It was also time to form just one group, not two. Leadership guru Jim Collins *(Good to Great and Fast Company)* clearly indicates that to move from being a good organisation to a great one requires a series of conscious choices and the discipline to follow those choices through. High in priority is the importance of 'getting the right people on the bus' and preferably sitting in the right seats. In the world of business this can happen by courtesy of the chequebook; in the world of school leadership, you need patience and awareness.

Collins also introduced leaders to the concept of the 'flywheel'. An organisation is like a massively heavy flywheel which will not move just by you, the leader, pushing it. There is a need to harness the whole organisation behind the push until it starts to move and gathers its own momentum. Doing that is not just the product of an imaginative programme for change; it is the consequence of grasping the sense of unity and purpose and putting in enormous energy to un-stick the rusted flywheel.

Once the leadership team is on the same bus, with the will and energy to get the flywheel moving, you can start to sort out what direction to take. Collins emphasises this point – people first, direction later. It was not until the unified leadership team was in place that we could start to evolve a school development plan that made any sense. Even then, the plan had considerable elasticity. Until everyone starts to move together in a certain direction you will not necessarily know what you are going to have to overcome. Impediments and difficulties, like rocks scattered below the ocean surface, are not commonly mapped out in advance. So any plan for development must have considerable flexibility, and as the leader you must be adaptable enough to alter course (see chapter 4).

Leading from the vision of Oneness, harnessing the emotional intelligence of the right people, and pointing everyone in the same direction, as attractive as it sounds, is not without its pitfalls or difficulties. The road can be full of potholes and tripwires, so leading in this way requires an understanding of what the obstacles are.

One senior colleague clearly felt undervalued and poorly utilised. His self-perception resembled that of Mr Chips without the burden of accuracy, and he resented not being given a leadership seat on the bus. He was in fact a brilliant classroom teacher, but was unwilling to put in the leadership work beyond a limited measure. When the rest of your team have put their clocks away and are doing whatever the job demands, it is disruptive to have someone pulling the other way: the prospect for division is high in such situations. In this case, a senior role was found – and one that absolutely suited his nature and which he was very good at – but which required neither excessive time nor much involvement with other leadership colleagues. The groaning remained, but the frequent one-to-one meetings maintained a measure of mutual respect and communication. My role was not to adopt a fixed and firm opinion of the individual, but to keep patiently waiting for something to change, and then to embrace it when it did. I needed to keep faith that it would come, and I needed somehow to find ways of communicating that faith. After nearly seven years of work, a change did take place and he became more open to what being on the leadership bus really meant. He took on extra tasks and became more positive, opening new possibilities for the future. Leading by the policy of Oneness does not mean you have to agree to everything – far from it! But you do have to keep trying.

The emotional intelligence approach can also sometimes be criticised for failing to provide 'directive leadership' (see chapter 7) – giving people specific directions to be followed. 'You are simply not telling us what we should be doing,' one staffer ranted in my office. 'No', I replied, 'I am asking you to truly meet the boys in front of you, understand what they need, and then use your immense intelligence to provide it.' Many people simply want to be told what to do most of the time (until it is something they don't want to do). There are certainly times when such an approach is needed and useful, but to move the bus in the direction you want, with everyone comfortably on it, such a directive style should only be used as an emergency measure.

Another pothole to cross is the accusation that the emotionally intelligent leader takes his decisions by pulling together everyone else's ideas, creating a blancmange of thought. By trying to satisfy all, he ends up satisfying none. Again, this is not how leadership, inspired by Oneness, operates. The key is to listen carefully to as many ideas as possible; where someone other than yourself clearly has the better idea and the knowledge to apply it, delegate the authority and give him the space to act. If there is no such person available, use your intuition to decide on the right course and then explain to the rest of the bus why you have chosen to do what you have done. It is explanation, and the time taken to give it, that keeps unity intact.

Finally, there is the staffroom cynic. He usually sits in the same place every day, drinking from the same mug and sniggering in the same way at comments either you or a member of your team may make. He has certainly seen it all before, or thinks he has, and wonders why all this management and leadership stuff matters in the least. He may profess to be independent, but when an issue he doesn't like comes up in the staffroom he lets you know that 'many of us' feel the same way. It is perhaps the most divisive, and the most difficult, situation to deal with, and based on discussion with fellow heads, nearly every school has at least one such character, if not several, lurking in the staffroom. Again, the key is holding to your own understanding of unity. He really is not different from you, at least in essence. His perceptions are different; so too are his thoughts and feelings – but try, as Jesus put it, to 'love him as your self'. This does not mean agreeing with him; it does not mean accommodating him. It means you always stay civil; you always try to greet him warmly and without internal prejudice. You keep smiling and patiently hope that one day he will change. Such hope keeps heads alive.

## Exercises for Cultivating Unity and Oneness

### Smile

As you walk around the school, consciously breathing and mindfully aware of all around you, ensure that you maintain at least a half smile on your face at all times. As you enter the staffroom for your regular briefing, pause at the door and no matter how you feel internally, put a smile on your face. Try to do this consistently.

The benefit of this approach is two-fold: your colleagues, noticing your smile, start to do the same (no matter how *they* are feeling); and you personally radiate your own inner happiness. (Happiness is always present – it just gets hidden.)

### Meeting Ice-breaker

Before leaping into an agenda of many items, spend a few minutes asking colleagues at a meeting to say something positive about their experience during the past week. What has been the highlight? What has brought a smile to their face? What has made them happy? This simple exercise changes atmospheres and energies in meetings, as it starts the agenda on a pleasant and positive footing.

If more time allows (say, at an inset day), divide people into small groups and give them a question that will bring out the best in them. Try one question that works exceptionally well, especially at the beginning of the academic year; for example, 'So, why did you become a teacher?' Then find some time to share the responses. It builds a real sense of purpose and reminds everyone why they are there.

### Developing Intuition and Trust

The greater the sense of Oneness, the more intuition steps in to help the decision-making processes. Intuition is the territory of 'the Knower': it is our power of awareness bringing to the mind what is needed, when it is needed. The mind must be clear, creating space for intuition to produce the knowledge required.

*Practice Stopping Regularly:* At the beginning and end of every activity, give yourself a few moments to *stop*. Feel your feet on the ground or your body on the chair. Open the sense of listening, and listen right out to the furthermost sound. Become aware of your inner breathing. Then just *watch* what is presented to the mind. Whatever it is, let it pass and keep watching. Regular practice of this exercise, sometimes called *The Pause*, opens the internal space and clears the mind of clutter.

*Trusting the Knowledge:* Having stopped and paused, the mind will present many things. Which is the knowledge you need? There are some telltale signs. First, it will tend to be unexpected. Second, it will frequently be obvious, but only once you have seen it. Third, it will always be full of common sense too. (If it is outrageous, chances are it has arisen from an imaginative centre, not real intuition.)

For one to be able to trust this knowledge, it has to be put into action. You have to step out into the unknown! Actually, intuition doesn't take a holiday. It is always working. It tells you when to call a family member, even if he or she is abroad and you haven't spoken together in ages; it tells you somebody wants something from you. Follow it. Gain confidence by finding out that your family member really did want to hear from you; that your colleague really did want to get something from you. Once confidence in the smaller things grows, it will be there in the larger things too. The intuition of the Knower is the leader's best friend.

# Chapter 4

# Leading From Behind

I KNEW I SHOULDN'T HAVE looked at the mobile phone flashing the message that my deputy wanted to speak to me. Right now. The problem was, I was addressing a training conference of aspiring head-teachers at the time, and we hadn't even started the bit about crisis management.

'And so, ladies and gentlemen', I remember telling the conference as I hastened to wrap up and get off the stage, 'one of the best things about headship is that you just never know what is about to happen to you. All you can really do is be prepared, stay calm, and follow any event as it unfolds'. I thanked the audience for their attention, apologised for not taking many questions, and dashed to a safe room to return the missed calls – countless instances of them by now.

'You will never guess who I am standing with in your office', my deputy said when I finally got in touch with him.

'No, surprise me', I said. 'The President of the United States?'

'Very funny', he retorted. 'It's even better. I am standing here with two esteemed members of the Metropolitan Police Service from Paddington nick, Art and Antiques division'. Thank God for small mercies! It could have been a child-protection issue.

'Uniformed or plain clothes?' I asked. It is always important to try to figure out immediately what others might be thinking – or who might be tweeting whom before you wake up to the fact that a perception problem took shape right in the middle of your office. After all, how many people saw them coming in? And where did they park their car?

'Plain', he said, cryptically.

'Why are they here and who have they come to see?'

'They haven't come to see anybody. They've come to arrest Mr X. They reckon he's been nicking valuable manuscripts and ancient texts from some of the best libraries'. And I thought the man was asking for time off for professional development courses. Some development!

'Have they got a warrant?'

'Yes, and they want to take him now'.

'They can't do that. It's not break time'. I desperately tried to joke, my mind racing over how this would look to the school community and how the chap himself would take it. The icy silence on the end of the phone quickly communicated that my pathetic attempt at humour and buying time was failing.

'They want me to get him out of the classroom now and bring him to your office, where they will read him his rights and arrest him'.

'Okay, but do it quickly and quietly', I proffered. 'I am coming straight back'.

Within the hour I had returned to school and the place was, well, buzzing with excitement. Despite the fact that no one had said anything, and no one had apparently *seen* anything, the sixth form had written on their classroom blackboard – right at the other end of the school – 'X in jail!' Just how do they do it?

You can't plan for this kind of thing. There is no head teacher's manual on how to react to a totally random critical incident. All you can do is *be there!* Be as present in the moment as you can possibly be – and follow the events.

Recourse to stillness in a situation like this is a heaven-sent blessing. Your mind races headlong towards all the things that might happen, and if you are not careful, what needs to be done simply escapes you. Brief the staff. Say nothing to the boys, at least not yet. Wait until you have more information. And, oh yes, don't forget to tell the chap's wife (or husband, as the case may be) that he won't be home for dinner. Send someone round to be with her and help her cope with the shock. Have a couple of lines up your sleeve in case the press get hold of the story, and prepare to send an email to the parents of all the students, just as soon as you know what you can say. Don't forget to tell the Chairman of Governors and the bursar. Send someone to the off-licence to get a few bottles of wine to help change the mood in the staffroom at the end of the day.

Knowing what to do is the territory of the Knower – the inner intelligence we all have, which works brilliantly in the present moment, but which so often gets covered by mental agitation and movement. Part of the ego mind wants to be in control and wants to get everything organized. 'I didn't plan for this', is a phrase the head's mind could repeat a hundred times a day. That is why I recommend establishing a new paradigm for headship: *cultivate the ability to lead by following events.*

Before delving more deeply into this, one misconception needs to be demolished. Leading from behind, or by *following* events, does not mean you are not seen to be at the front and centre, taking charge when you need to be. In fact, leading from behind is where you become so present to the moment, so in tune with the now, so awake and aware of what is happening all around you that the Knower tells you what to do *before* anybody else has woken up to what is happening. External observers would think you are not *following*, but are right out in front, setting the pace and the agenda. You don't need to disabuse them of the idea. But within yourself, you know you are waiting, you are watching, and only when it is clear (which it will be very quickly) are you acting.

Not only is this technique ideal in a crisis, but it is also a brilliant way to lead in a more general sense. Your wakefulness and calmness are just as vital in a normal day as an exceptional one. If you listen to colleagues they will clearly tell you what is happening; and by getting into the present moment – by retuning into the Knower – the right way to go and whose voice to follow will be abundantly evident.

When the governors asked, not unreasonably, for a three-year development plan, I produced a very short one in the full knowledge that it would never materialise, especially the way people thought it might. Several general principles and ideas were set, but the details would have to wait for events to unfold. Over the next three years, our situation became so different from what it had been at the beginning that fresh, new solutions were needed, which simply could not have been thought of in advance.

For the kind of person who prides himself on the perfection of planning, down to the last detail, it is not comfortable to lead in this way. Of course, well-organised plans often work, but how sterile they are by comparison to an approach that is living and dynamic and adaptable to change based on what is going on NOW. A recording of Mozart's *The Magic Flute* can bring great joy, but when you see it performed on stage, hear the music live, and smell the scent of Papageno, let alone the Queen of the Night, the vibrancy heightens and the joy is magnified. Leading from behind brings everything in leadership alive and activates the Knower, which magnifies the freshness and inspires creativity.

We are all forced into making plans, but why do we expect circumstances to happen accordingly when so often they don't? In headship, your diary might say one thing but the chance of all the events taking place as scheduled is remote. Another approach is possible. We can think of the general outline of an action plan that points us in the right direction, but resist filling in the detail until the moment arrives. All too frequently we lack the self-confidence to follow the events that are right in front of us. A doubt creeps into our minds that if we haven't organised everything in advance, we are going to stumble and make a complete idiot of ourselves. In fact, the reality is usually the other way round. Making a plan and sticking slavishly to it can lead to the gravest of mistakes and, more importantly, missed opportunities.

Shortly after I took the headship at St James, our school community found itself embroiled in an ugly argument with former pupils who felt the regime of corporal punishment they had endured during their studies had been too harshly applied. The rulebook on how to deal with this kind of complaint was written in invisible ink, but about a dozen UK schools faced similar problems and, as far as we could tell, those problems were not going away. A new response was needed, but what was it?

The risks to the reputation of the school caused by doing nothing (always a potential strategy to consider) were too great and yet there was no clear course of action. A colleague and I met an action group of former pupils, who impressed us with their grievances. The balance of emotion and reason was decidedly lacking in their expression, but they felt hurt and something needed to be done to address their pain.

An adventurous governor focussed on one question: How do we find out the truth of what took place? He quoted from The Bible, 'The truth will set you free', and argued amongst his colleagues that simply establishing the truth would lead to justice and alleviate the students' emotional pain. The more intent the Board became on the issue, the more we refined possible courses of action, until a totally innovative and never-before-tried solution came to light: hold an independent 'public enquiry'. It was a bold move which could have back-fired spectacularly. But as the governor told his colleagues, the greater risk was that the truth would never be revealed and innocent parties would be blamed and damaged, along with the reputation of the school. It takes guts to open yourself up, but in this case, the result of doing so was that a powerful determination arose to face the situation and deal with it, once and for all.

A prominent Queen's Counsel was found to hear the case of the aggrieved former students, and the masters involved were given ample opportunity to tell their side of the story, including the former headmaster. Much to everyone's relief, he was exonerated from any personal malpractice or inappropriate use of the cane (saved by the evidence of his 'punishment book' – a key document in the drawer of every headmaster). A handful of other teachers, many of whom had long retired, found themselves criticised for the way they had exercised corporal punishment. Three teachers currently on staff were sanctioned, all of whom had clean records apart from the incidents that had taken place thirty years earlier, and the reasonable course was to reprimand and warn, not sack them.

Every step along the way was new. No one had ever done what we were doing before. Very few had attempted to bring inner peace to a group of vociferous opponents of a school that had clearly changed in keeping with the times. The whole sorry saga had to be *followed,* and with courage. The lead governor, at the end of it all, then launched a reconciliation process which he has doggedly pursued for several years. His Intent (see chapter 5) remained focussed and clear – to settle the minds and hearts of anyone who thought he had been hurt or harmed by a system of education that involved corporal punishment. His leadership approach was just to follow events as they unfolded, day by day and hour by hour. Today, the vast majority of complainants have recognised the huge value in the process and acknowledged that they were helped to see the whole situation (see chapter 2) in a new way.

It takes a certain kind of inner resilience to lead from behind, because your consciousness, the Knower, will let you see things you might wish were not there at all. The blind leader may rest in some form of ignorant bliss by not seeing trouble ahead, but eventually the thundercloud claps and the downpour begins. It is best to either avert the storm if you can, or at least get a proper raincoat to cope with it.

Preparing for such storms so that events can be followed, day after day, is described in the field of emotional intelligence as cultivating self-management. I prefer to call it 'personal mastery'.

Personal mastery is nothing new. Plato called it 'temperance' and declared it to be one of four cardinal virtues alongside courage, justice, and wisdom. To be temperate was to exercise self-control, avoid excess, and remain even-minded, especially in the midst of difficulties. Eastern philosophers have a beautiful word to describe the same state: *samadhi*. This is not only the state of the enlightenment; levels of it can be experienced and benefited from in daily life. In Sanskrit, the word *sam* means 'even' and *dhi* means 'intellect'. So *samadhi* is the quality of the mind that shines with the uncoloured, pre-existing knowledge of self and how things really are. It shines brightest when the mind is still and even, like a placid lake reflecting the moon.

Personal mastery doesn't quite work without the taste of stillness – not just the stillness at the beginning and end of an event like that provided by a conscious *Pause*, (see the exercises at the end of this chapter), but throughout. To expect that state of inner calm to descend upon you without practice is like expecting to run a marathon after doing no more preparation than walking to the shops every other weekend. Real personal mastery occurs when the mind remembers the *samadhi* state, the state of evenness, as often as possible and dedicates some time to finding it daily.

One young banker, a former pupil, told the story of how he had found himself in a typhoon of activity: the company he was tracking announced a drop in profits when everyone was expecting an increase.

'Instantly, I knew there must have been a mistake somewhere in the system', he told a group of wide-mouthed Year 11s, all hoping for a crack at the big pay cheque themselves.' The trading floor went bonkers, with everyone shouting at me wanting to know what to do. The only thing I knew at that moment was not to move, not to take a decision, not to tell them anything. I knew I had to wait'. And so he did – for nearly a full two minutes, an enormous length of time in the midst of frenzied trading activity. Then just as suddenly as before, news came again: a mistake had been made in a press release. The company had actually made a profit and instead of selling, the profitable course of action was to buy. The frenzy of panic-selling had forced the price to drop artificially low, and so the young banker's buy command to his traders meant they cleaned up, big time. 'So how much did you make?' one of our youngsters asked.' About ten million dollars', the banker rather sheepishly replied. He had kept his cool. He said he had learnt this at school by stopping and pausing before the beginning and end of every lesson. He had personal mastery and he had never forgotten the technique. Nor did the Year 11s.

Personal mastery is the secret to dealing with stress. Learning how to follow events is the secret to personal mastery, and that in turn requires an ability to manage our moods.

Like it or not, our moods can easily get the better of us. The late night finance and estates meeting where the bursar simply has no clue of what you really want can cause more than a flutter in the head's mind next morning, usually taken out on some poor and unsuspecting pupil or staff member. Mary in the English department did not deserve that scowl, which crossed your face when you passed her in the corridor because your mind had drifted back to the night before. Yes, our thoughts are read on our faces and in the slump of our bodies. By nearly everybody.

The precondition to successful mood management is, first, to be aware of what we are feeling and what our mind is contemplating at all times. Most of us have a well-established pattern of moods which those closest to us know all too well. The triggers for those moods are usually the same kinds of things, and if we are honest with ourselves, most of the triggers have produced the same kinds of reactions since we were at school. The cycle is the product of our past actions and behaviours – what Hindus sometimes call 'karma' or what Jesus described simply as reaping the results of the seeds we have sown. If you have found yourself in a miserable mood each time you haven't got your way, and you have practised this repeatedly, then the bad mood is certainly going to descend when any similar trigger is galvanised.

Stepping back and reflecting inwardly on what triggers our less than charming moods is a kind of self-reflection thoroughly to be recommended, because the leader cannot afford to be swung from pillar to post by patterns from the past. He has to find his way back to the present. Having undertaken this kind of reflection, he can adopt alternative practices, such as expressing the opposite emotions, which can then become second nature.

*The Smile* (see chapter 3) is one such exercise; others are listed at the conclusion of this chapter.

Early on in my headship I met my first parent from hell. I had heard such creatures existed but never believed they could be quite so testing. I woke up to the fact that, if anything, my new colleagues had been downplaying their dreadfulness.

'You are a novice at this head-mastering, totally ill-prepared and incompetent', she declared within minutes of the start of the meeting. Instead of letting it pass, and instead of recognising and heeding all the signs of my own tiredness and irritation, I could not help but react.

'And I see you are as poorly behaved as your son', the smart alec in me retorted, allowing myself a half smile before she took out the howitzer.

Governor appeals panels, formal complaints procedures, threats of going to the press (such parents are nearly always 'connected' to the media, or so they say) – the potential wrath of God descended. Far from *following* the event, I tried to manipulate it and found myself in hotter water by the mouthful. My mother had always warned me about my temper, which I usually let loose on opponents on the football field, resulting in the occasional red card. I knew it was troublesome and so worked hard for many years with daily meditation and breathing to bring it under control, successfully, I thought, until the meeting with this parent.

I made a second classic mistake, as well: I did not have another colleague with me, armed with pen and paper, to write notes and to intervene if the situation got particularly bad.

My whole body was reacting. I felt possessed by some strange agitating force that was causing, in the midst of my tiredness, not only loss of self-control, but even the loss of basic good manners and politeness. Fortunately, after what seemed an age and a torrent of her continuing abuse, I mustered up the strength to apologise.

'I am very sorry to have insulted you', I said. 'I have made a mistake and I will try to learn from this'. I felt terrible at one level, but the result of the apology was to regain some of my personal mastery. The knowledge of what to do next was clear – terminate the meeting as fast as possible and go home. Within minutes, she stood up, slammed the door as she went out, opened it again to apologise for the loud noise, and finally left the school premises. Personal mastery is essential, and even she had regained some of it at the end.

Dealing with such events can be extremely stressful, particularly if they repeat in quick succession, as they so often seem to do. Learning to follow events, however, gives some respite for the weary and eases the ruffling pushes and pulls. The simple reason for this is that you are not trying to achieve a particular outcome and are therefore more open to what is likely to happen. This openness is thoroughly to be recommended.

In the Bhagavad Gita, a seminal text in Hinduism, the mighty warrior and archer, Prince Arjuna, takes to the battlefield with his guru, Lord Sri Krishna, acting as his charioteer. Arjuna is depressed because he doesn't want to fight his friends and extended family, and the two characters engage in an extraordinary discussion on the nature of work and happiness. Krishna proffers two pieces of remarkably good advice; a head teacher could think he had head teachers in mind when he delivered it.

First, he tells Arjuna to attend to his duty with no desire for personal reward. 'Work for the work's sake', he said, 'and any fruits of the work should be handed back to God, the source of all energy and intelligence'. The moral was clear: get on with what you have to do but recognise that the divine powers are coursing through your veins at every step. It is not you, the ego, who is brilliant – it is You the Knower, the God-force within you, living in your heart. Then Krishna tells Arjuna to acknowledge that power of God in the midst of action: don't *think* of yourself as the doer of the action alone, but rather, acknowledge yourself as the instrument of God in the action. Both of these steps are conducive to *samadhi*, evenness of mind or personal mastery, and from it considerable happiness naturally arises along with the relief of stress.

Stress comes upon us when we let our minds drift from the present moment. We often look outside of ourselves for the causes of stress, but the rather sobering feature is that stress is largely internally generated. We worry about what is going to happen. We worry about how we might meet it. We remember the times we got things wrong in the past and fret that we might repeat our actions. Every time we fear for the future or regret the past we are out of the present moment and therefore cannot follow the event. At such times we cannot lead by *following*. It is not the events that are the source of stress – it is our internal considerations. Stress is mind-induced.

One criticism of this approach of leading from behind is that it is too passive; that it envisions the head sitting happily on a deck chair as the ship sinks beneath him, remembering that the cause of it all is God and that He is really the one to blame. But this is not what I am suggesting at all. The proposal is to act *after* you have seen what is needed – not *before* you have seen what is needed. When acting, acknowledge the Knower within you who is guiding and directing your considerable intelligence, and claim nothing at the end.

None of this approach can work without a considerable inner strength, and that comes from self-knowledge in the first instance and an awakening awareness in the second. Assuming both have been established, and assuming that you grasp the practice of seeing whoever you are dealing with as no one other than yourself, the ground-rules for leading by *following*, and having the self-confidence to do so, are very much in place.

One night, rather late, my wife and I were asleep when we heard an enormous bang, followed by the sound of smashing glass and a thud. I rushed downstairs to find a brick on the hall floor, and without any forensics, I knew that it had the fingerprints of the boy I had expelled that afternoon all over it. The scene wasn't funny, but the policeman who came to investigate could not constrain a wry smile when I told him my occupation and my suspicions. 'Well sir, just be grateful you didn't expel Osama bin Laden's son', he wisecracked. I couldn't help feeling compassion for the lad, a sentiment not fully shared by my poor wife, who'd had not just her sleep destroyed, but her sense of personal safety too. At such times, personal mastery is important, because the event has to be followed if you are to be of any help to the people involved.

In this case, the lad was pursued by the police and social services. Help was provided, but finally the courts had to impose an antisocial behaviour order (ASBO). I couldn't help feeling a sense of failure. Equally, however, the job demands that such feelings not be dwelt on for too long. Heads have to learn how to recover quickly; and fortunately, the job lets you do so because tomorrow is going to be full of new and fresh challenges, most of which you could never plan for. Actually, leading from behind and *following* the events is the only sane way to proceed; that is, if you want to stay free of enormous personal burdens. Personal mastery replaces such burdens and sets you free to follow – which is the real secret of leading.

## Exercises to Grow in Personal Mastery and Follow Events

### The Pause

This is an ancient exercise practised by many professionals, particularly those who must appear frequently on stage or in public. Regular practice of *The Pause*, before the beginning of an activity and at the end of it (before moving on to the next one), creates a sense of *sam*, evenness and personal mastery.

1. Start simply by feeling your feet on the floor.
2. Now feel your body on the chair and the clothes on your body.
3. Follow the breath as it moves in and out of the body. Take your time for this.
4. Open the ears.
5. Listen to the immediate sounds, and let them pass.
6. Listen to the more distant sounds, and let them pass.
7. Now stretch the listening to embrace the silence that surrounds all sounds. Linger here until your attention moves.

This practice is best done with eyes closed, but if you wish to keep them open, add one step before step 4: allow the impressions of colour and form to enter the field of vision and let them pass. Always end with listening.

### Mood Management

There are several steps to this exercise. They can be practised over a series of days or weeks.

1. The first step is the practice of *deep honesty*. Sit back, reflect on what moods overcome you in what circumstances, and write them down.

2. The second step is to show what you have written down to your partner or your best friend as a reality check. Discuss what you have written down openly. Try to avoid being defensive.

3. The third step is to take each mood and give it your focussed attention for a period, say a day or two. *Just watch the mood. Do nothing else with it. Watch.* While you watch the mood as an objective observer (which is in fact the Knower) it will begin to fade away. Let it fade. If you keep doing this regularly, it will finally go away altogether.

## Drifting – Just Follow Events

Just *following* events is sometimes described as 'drifting' or going with the flow.

This is largely a mental conditioning, rather than a 'doing' of something.

Establish a day in the diary where you are just going to *drift* – rather like a piece of driftwood. Keep your diary free of all set appointments. Allow yourself to roam to any part of the school, wherever the Knower takes you.

Throughout this exercise, you must keep practicing *The Smile* and keep watching the movements of your mind. Let everything go and just flow.

This is a remarkably testing exercise, so you might want to start with shorter half-day periods. You should also recognise that this exercise needs to be done two or three times before you will become sufficiently at ease with yourself to get the benefits.

At the end of every day or period of *Drifting* note down what you experienced. When you have written a few entries, compare them to your notes on *Mood Management.* The comparison is extremely informative and will help you both to deepen your practice of *Drifting* and manage your moods. You will also feel very much less stressed.

### Reducing the Angles of Stress

Stress increases as our attention moves away from the present moment – the now.

The distance between the present moment and our dreams about the future or regrets about what has passed is what I call the angle of stress.

The practice is to keep coming back into the present moment as often as possible, thereby reducing the angle of stress.

Regular practice of *The Pause* before and at the end of every activity is exceptionally helpful in this.

## ANGLES OF STRESS

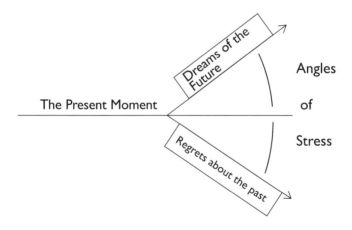

# CHAPTER 5

# PUSHING OUR BEST BUTTONS

W E ALL HAVE CERTAIN POSITIVE buttons within us which, when pushed, bring out the best we have to offer. These buttons are not on the surface of our minds but are to be found deep in the inner core of ourselves, right in the centre of our hearts. In leadership terms, they constitute *intent*. Not surprisingly, they are concerned with what we love and what we think we have been put here to do.

Our intent connects us with our inner power to achieve anything we want. This connection keeps us going, especially when times get tough. Our intent also keeps us on track, and when fully discovered, allows for a great expansion of inner fulfilment and satisfaction. And after all, is that not what life is ultimately all about?

But there's an immediate catch. That satisfaction, whilst intensely personal, also needs to be made fully available to everyone you are serving; otherwise, it disappears – fast! Headship is all about service, and whilst there is no law against intense personal joy and happiness, experience quickly tells us that to make it last, it must be made into a shared experience.

The very best heads I know love to serve. Serving is one of their key buttons. Any aspiring head who can't find this button should stop thinking about the job immediately. The very best heads don't simply relish the power and position of their role. That is extraneous for them and if any new head should discover this to be a primary focus, he would be best advised to discard it quickly. Identification with the enormous power of the position brings to the fore all our inner demons, the very worst in us, and before we know where we have landed, trouble will not be far away. You should want the job not for what it can give you but for what you can give to it.

When the intent behind the role is simply to serve, a natural humility arises. Quite frequently I have heard heads express a sense of bewilderment as to how they got into the position in the first place. They couldn't always see in themselves what someone else could, and they took to the job naturally and with ease. Humility was a quality that was never far from them.

So often, modern leadership models portray a thrusting alpha character pushing all others to the side so that he can claim the top spot. In headship this is a quick route to disaster.

Jim Collins' research in *Good to Great and the Social Sectors* identified several characteristics in what he termed 'Level 5 leaders': leaders who have managed to build something well beyond themselves which lasted. These men and women possess two special qualities in power-pack form: humility and will. The Level 5 leader can certainly unfold a vision and pursue it by stimulating colleagues to perform with inspiration and results beyond what is expected; but that is not what makes them special. Their specialness is the very idea that they hold in themselves that they are not special! They are simply committed to serve.

Collins was asked to name, based on his research into what turned a good corporation into a great one, the most outstanding Level 5 organisations and leaders. The remarkable thing was that while the names of the organisations were certainly familiar (Hewlett Packard, 3M, Johnson & Johnson, Boeing Corporation), the names of the Level 5 leaders were not.

His own personal favourite Level 5 leader was a man named William Allen. I have to admit that I had never heard of him and had to do some research to find out about him. He was the Boeing Company president from the end of the war in 1945 until 1968, and he is credited with driving this manufacturer of old-fashioned bombers into the jet age, thus making it a household name. He wasn't an aviator – he was a lawyer – and he simply didn't think he was up to the job, a feeling I suspect that is rather familiar to many of us. The sudden loss of his childhood sweetheart opened a space in his life. That, combined with the challenge of what to do with an out-of-date warplane manufacturer employing thousands of people, intrigued him. For the sake of the company employees, he took on the role of president and started to develop what became known as the Boeing 707.

The day came for a public showing of this new and uncertain creation. But it was not Allen who took the glory seat – it was a test pilot called Tex Johnson. All was going well until Johnson decided, unannounced, to perform a barrel roll rather close to the ground. A stunned Allen, fearing that something had gone terribly wrong, felt the blood drain from his feet, but Johnson had just felt so enthusiastic that he wanted everyone to know exactly what the plane could do. Allen is reported to have commented at the time to Johnson, 'Don't ever do that to me again!' More than twenty years later, Allen admitted to an audience that he had been furious with the test pilot for risking all and that it had taken him years to begin to see the humour and brilliance in what he had done. It is interesting to note that today we know the name Boeing, but the name Allen is not familiar at all. It would never have crossed his mind to call it 'Allen Airlines'.

After those early post-war days, Boeing sold more than two thousand 707 airframes and developed the 737, 747, 757, 767, and 777, creating one of the world's most successful companies. William Allen, on the other hand, is remembered for the community service projects that he sponsored and stimulated every step of the way. Level 5 leaders leave a legacy, but it does not belong to their ego. It is an expression in the world of their true intent and humility.

What Collins calls 'will' I call 'intent'. It is the only thing that a man can change. In fact, without changing his intent nothing else can change. Whatever the intent, the action will follow it directly.

I remember the day in 1979 when the news was that around 200,000 Vietnamese refugees, the boat people, had been found, and a massive political row broke out in Mrs T's office about whether to shelter a number of them in the UK. The Conservative Party had recently released a manifesto committing to halt immigration, and there was an ugly right-wing smugness around parts of the Cabinet table. The prime minister was in an internal political bind.

My observation of her dealing with the issue made one thing very clear: it was her mothering instinct button that was coming to the fore, not her right-wing tendency. She had to speak to the media and to colleagues, but my inner feeling throughout that time was that the mother in her would not let desperate souls rot, no matter what the political fallout. Three weeks after the row erupted, a prime ministerial statement in the Commons announced that 19,000 boat people would be welcomed. Compassion and common sense had prevailed because that was her *will*.

Regrettably I never had the chance to meet the great Eric Anderson, former head master and provost of Eton College and, before that, head master of several of the country's finest schools. But from his actions you can tell something about his inner intent. During his early career, he taught Prince Charles at Gordonstoun. At Fettes College in Edinburgh he became Tony Blair's housemaster. Blair had Anderson in mind when he launched the 1997 advertising campaign by the Teacher Training Agency ('No one forgets a good teacher'). While Anderson was head master of Eton, David Cameron was there, as was Boris Johnson. You might write all this off by saying it is fate that one man should touch the lives of several of our most important leaders. More likely, however, it had something to do with the power of his intent.

If you intend to serve the highest principles in education and if you intend to care for the souls and hearts, as well as the minds and bodies, of your pupils, then you will find great pupils coming to you. It is your intent that is attractive, and it is your intent that will guide the actions which follow.

At St James Senior Boys' we put great value on the importance of Quiet Time and Meditation. It's a bedrock of what we do. On arriving here, however, I found that some senior staff had decided that any boy over the age of sixteen was psychologically challenged and could not be still; and therefore, it was totally wrong to oblige them to follow any meditative practice. Surely they were old enough to make up their own minds? A clash of wills was inevitable.

I examined my intent and it became perfectly clear to me that I would be failing if they were not given the chance to meditate with the other boys. As stillness is so comforting and stress-relieving, it seemed unreasonable that they might not want it. I took the view that someone else's intent had got in the way and it needed to change.

Exercising some directive leadership (see chapter 7), I created the opportunity in morning assemblies for every boy to be still and rest in his own peace for around ten minutes. Whatever any chap wanted to take from this or however he wanted to use the time was entirely up to him. He could meditate. He could practice awareness breathing exercises. He could pray. He could sit, watch the movements of his mind, and just be.

I decided we could exist on the foundation of one rule. Simplicity of rules is always very practical. The rule was, 'Do not disturb the peace of another man'. No 'shoulds' or 'should nots'. Just simple reason. I wanted the boys to experience something of what I had received in meditation for many years. The experience was deep in my heart and very important to me. It was a fundamental part of my intent, and I felt it right to share it.

At the start, our collective Quiet Time seemed to make no difference at all. The lads were at best reluctant and at worst disruptive in a few cases. I forced myself to keep trusting them and restrained myself (by a touch of personal mastery) from giving the traditional head master's rollicking if they misbehaved or moved. In fact, I tried to smile my way through. I was confident my will would overcome theirs.

Slowly, and still more slowly, the atmosphere in the assembly refined, and week by week the boys eased into a quieter inner space. Some of them even looked as if they were enjoying it and were really finding some peace.

Three years into the collective Quiet Time experiment, a group of sixth formers came to me and said something that was absolutely music to my ears: they wanted to volunteer to mentor the new Year 7 chaps, not only in academic work, but in meditation practice as well. It was an enormous breakthrough. As I reflected on how it happened, it became clear that as each month passed, a few more supporters embraced the intent behind the Quiet Time practice. A volunteer helper appeared who loved to meditate and could see how the young men would benefit. He started to mentor them, and they in turn picked up the idea. A senior colleague came to me repeatedly to say how, despite the negative reactions in certain quarters, the Quiet Time experiment should continue. He then determined to fully support it in his own area. It is not really possible to fulfil your intent without such support.

The message to new heads from this account is that nothing is impossible. If your intent, whatever it is, really matters to you, keep going with it. Be patient. Be gently persistent. The inner forces within you will be released and somehow the outer forces will come to your aid. Never give up on finding ways to fulfil your intent.

Your intent is the catalyst to the unfolding of your vision, another button an aspiring head must find and push. If intent is a matter of the emotional ground, then vision is a matter of the mind. The word vision implies seeing something grand. Much is made of the importance of vision in modern leadership, but actually, vision is subsidiary to your intent. Your intent can last a lifetime, whereas a vision may just last a few minutes. Those few minutes, however, can shape days and months of activity.

One early spring evening in 2009, the telephone rang with news that was to dramatically change all of our lives at St James Senior Boys'. A girls' school relatively nearby was in financial trouble, and the trustees wanted to know if we might be interested in making an arrangement for some kind of merger. The trustees, in the very best interests of British education stretching back more than 300 years, were bound by covenants which meant they could not sell off their assets without first seeking to find another compatible educational institution to partner with. Their hope had been to link with a girls' school, but if that was not possible, a boys' school with a compatible ethos would be fine.

I had never visited the school before but decided later that evening to drive out to see it. The imposing wrought-iron gates did not mask the impressive mid-19th century building, which, through squinted eyes, looked somewhat like J K Rowling's Hogworts. In front of the three-floor Gothic facade was a beautiful playing field bordering on a lake, just a part of the 32 acres of playing fields. The more I peered at the fields, the more I could see rugby goal posts sticking up. Of course, they weren't really there, but in my mind was flashing a vision of what could happen if we were to occupy the site.

Shortly after starting discussions with our board of governors, it became clear that our girls' school would not be able to move and make use of the premises, but our own boys' school certainly could. The prospective partners admired our educational philosophy and found it compatible with the will and intent of their own founders, and within six weeks an agreement had been reached. The girls' school on the site would fold and a boys' school – complete with rugby posts on the front fields – would replace it. The vision was unfolding.

Medical research has begun to discover the essential link between the state of the mind and the state of the body. I would propose the same is true in leadership of any kind. Powered by your intent, with your vision lighting the way, the leader can proceed to unfold what is most important to him in a way that best meets the needs of those he is leading. As the Buddha said, 'As you think, so it will be.'

Working like this is not without conflicts and pressures. This is where an understanding is essential of what, in my work with young leaders, I have called the *decision tree.*

Each branch of the decision tree represents a step in a leader's ability to look towards the larger picture and to put the needs of those he is serving before his own (see diagram below). When considering decisions he must take, if all he thinks about is his immediate family, he will stop any course of action that might create a conflict between their needs and his own. The same applies if he is concerned only about his immediate community (such as the school he presides over) or the wider community (the town or area).

The majority of decisions never create conflicts, but frequently the important ones do.

While pursuing my career in business, I met a number of charismatic and dynamic characters. I chatted with some of them over a glass of wine or two about the value of a political career either alongside or after their business life. One of the people, who became a personal friend, held a high position in a leading American pharmaceutical company. He was brilliant with words, his decision-making was sharp, and he was the kind of person who naturally attracted others and easily generated a sense of trust and confidence.

At the time, the Republican Party was struggling to find candidates for the Senate and the House of Representatives, let alone presidential hopefuls. A group of party supporters started a minor campaign to convince my friend to consider running for the Senate and then, if all went well, the presidency. He was flattered and excited, and once that had worn off, he became serious about the possibilities. Media advisers, fundraisers, and policy consultants thought he had a good chance of succeeding; and he felt that he could clearly see what the country needed, especially in terms of economic development.

'Come on', I told him one night during dinner at the Hay Adams Hotel in Washington, which looks imperiously out over the White House. 'You know your country needs men like you. You know you can do it. Why are you hesitating?'

His answer was understandable, and it stopped him in his tracks. 'I don't want to put my children through all that. And my wife is not happy with the prospect of my spending less time with the family'.

The work-life balance is a critical thing in any leadership role. But if you are going to climb the decision tree, it is important to work out how to take the family along with you. In this case, my friend did not feel he could do this. He could not climb more than a couple of branches up the decision tree. 'I just can't leave the children', he told me.

In reality, his intent to serve his immediate family, wonderful at its own level, was more powerful than his intent to serve his country. It is an obstacle many people face that frequently leads to career frustration. My friend had to tell his political backers to look for someone else to run for the Senate, which, without hesitation, they did. Unfortunately, they missed out on having an outstanding man serve his political community, as did the United States as a whole.

I am certainly not arguing here for abandoning your family and selfishly chasing your own career path at all costs. The principle of the decision tree is that if you serve the highest level possible, then all the levels beneath it will get the attention they need and will be fully taken care of. You need intelligence to do this, as well as a fair degree of trust and faith. But in my own experience leading groups, it works. Above all else, what works is communicating to your family not only what you are doing, but also why you are doing it. This means opening yourself up and sharing with those closest and dearest to you what truly inspires and motivates you; in other words, revealing your intent and vision to those you love.

As my business life unfolded and became more successful, my travel commitments increased. I was teaching adult courses in philosophy, and this too required extensive travel. Either of these commitments would have put a strain on the family, but both happening simultaneously created real domestic pressure. I resolved to do two things: always tell the children why I had to go away and ensure that I phoned and spoke to each child, and my wife, every day, no matter where I was in the world. Today, my three sons are successful businessmen in their own rights, and I am delighted to see that they care for our grandchildren thoroughly, in every way. They have not abandoned their families; they have embraced them in their greater intent and vision, and they work high up in the decision tree.

The highest place to serve on the decision tree is the where you serve humanity as a whole. That sounds very grand, but it is in fact what every teacher does every day of his or her life. In front of every teacher or head is a representative collection of the human race. Teachers know this, and it is for this reason that we chose the role. It is also for this reason that our work in education is much more than a job – it is a vocation.

A vocation is a calling from the Divine. I have found that a real teacher strives to bring forth the brilliance of every child. When this is done in the true spirit of *educare*, the Latin word from which we get our word 'education', the glory of the Creative Force is clearly manifest. If a child becomes great in himself or herself and grows up to serve his society, to care for his family, and to make a real contribution, his teacher has served humanity at the highest level on the decision tree.

Robert Greenleaf termed this 'servant leadership', an idea that has swept the corridors of modern leadership development. Greenleaf himself was the kind of humble leader, filled with a fierce resolve to lift the human spirit, that Jim Collins described as a Level 5 leader. He abhorred the cult status of modern leadership gurus, and in 1988, two years before his death at age eighty-six, forbade the showing of a simple video about his life at the first symposium on Servant Leadership. At the age of sixty-six, he wrote an essay based on his observations during his long career at the American corporate giant, AT&T. He sent the article to a younger business friend, who began to circulate copies through his company. More and more people copied the essay and passed it on. (This was an early form of viral marketing.) It wasn't until he was seventy-three that he turned his thoughts into a full-scale book.

Greenleaf's biographer, Don Frick, wrote that his mentor 'heeded inner promptings of intuition, prepared himself without always knowing the goal of his preparation, gained much of his learning from astonishing people and always remained a seeker. He lived servant leadership before he ever defined it.' (*Robert K Greenleaf*, by Don Frick) The core idea of servant leadership, he says, is quite simple: '... authentic, ethical leaders, those whom we trust and want to follow, are servants first. This is a matter of intent, action, skills, capacities and being.'

The last part of that – the condition of being – is essential in servant-leadership, which is why the leader must be prepared to work on all aspects of himself – physically, mentally, emotionally, and spiritually (see chapter11). We are usually so focussed on the effectiveness of our 'doing' that our 'being' can easily be forgotten. Greenleaf makes being integral to the description of the successful servant-leader because the state of being is intimately connected to our intent.

When examining my intent on taking up headship, I got a great shock. Up until then, my intent had not included all the people I was leading and serving, only some. I had my favourites, even though I told myself I didn't. They were the ones who always supported what I said and did. They were the ones who I thought looked after me. But after some time, that level of intent was not enough. I took a careful look at things in the quietude of my own meditation. After all, if I could not be true to myself alone, in the depths of my own being, to whom could I be true?

The ancient prayer, 'May all be happy', used by Mandela at his inauguration (see chapter 1), is the best description of what a spiritual and practical intent should be about. Why would I want only some of the children to be happy or only some of the staff? And should not the parents be included? Why do parents have to be regarded just as 'customers'? That is a less than dignified term for those paying the bills at private schools and an obscene description of those sending pupils to state schools. Parents need to know they are true partners in the educational experience, as are the teachers, the pupils, the governors, the bursars, the maintenance team, the cleaners, the grounds staff, the kitchen staff, and the coach drivers. Many functions work harmoniously to make the modern school exceptional and happy.

This intent is known as the *ideal of Oneness,* the unity of all interests in which everybody is treated equally and appropriately. The aim is to love, respect, and serve the humanity existing in every person. It is a high ideal and, I have to admit, it is often not met. But the ideal remains, and, holding it, I wake up each morning remembering what the day before me is about. An intent that does not reflect the highest of human aspirations will fail to generate full satisfaction from the work at hand. This principle maintains that the largest truth – your own human *being* – cannot find satisfaction in anything less than itself.

In the business world, I came across many whose intent was a far cry from the welfare of the people. It was usually related to wealth, profit, or driving up the promotion ladder 'for me'. This frustrates young leaders because they often see such people succeeding in top jobs. When they point this out, I reply that such people might get the top jobs, but do they keep them? And are they really happy? Above all, do they have peace of mind? Whether you achieve the highest positions or not, if your intent is not giving you peace of mind and generating happiness for those you are serving, then it is worth an urgent review.

Peace of mind does not come from outer success; it arises from the sense of inner worth, which is generated from the knowledge that your skill, talent, and energy are being used in the service of humankind. The best heads I have met are those who are the most at peace with themselves, who are humble but at the same time fiercely resolved to get the best for their teachers, pupils, and parents, and who are capable of generating real happiness all around them.

When prospective parents go school-hunting , they usually have a number of must-haves on their shopping list. Underlying every item on the list is the happiness of their child. Happiness is the result of a true intent. If a person, however, works to achieve happiness just for himself, it will remain elusive. The intent must be happiness for all, not just for me.

Whether we fully realise it or not, the intent button is being pushed nearly every moment of our waking day. It is the force behind the way we approach whatever we do. It is subtle and powerful.

We need to see our intent clearly. For this we must continue to improve our level of awareness. Being you (see chapter 2) is very much about becoming comfortable with your own intent. If you are not comfortable, the reasonable approach is to change it. This is the real realm of change management.

## Exercises in Discovering Personal Intent

1. Go to a quiet spot without distractions, taking only a pen and paper.
2. Practise some breathing exercises to try and become as still as possible. Just watch the movement of the mind.
3. When you feel ready, present this question to your mind: "What do I love?" Watch the responses that appear and write them down. (Note: the question refers to 'what', not 'who.')
4. Spend no more than half an hour on this. Repeat the whole process ( steps 1-3) two or three times on subsequent days, noting the responses on the same sheet of paper.
5. At another time, examine the responses and look for common themes. The common themes will indicate the essence of your intent.

## Discovering the Intent of the Senior Management Team

1. Individuals attending an inset day can practise the exercise above and then share the results.
2. The leader may invite participants to look for common intents. Most team members share several intents but haven't always recognised this or discussed it.

Another team-based exercise starts with putting questions before the SMT.

1. Ask them: Who are we here to serve? What we are here to do? What unites us?
2. After some time for reflection, each member might answer one question in front of the others .
3. Take notes on the responses and see how much common ground exists between team members.

*Reflections on the Universal Prayer*

Below is the Sanskrit prayer that Nelson Mandela arranged to be sung at his inauguration as president of South Africa. It is a prayer for unity. It is a prayer for the world, for a nation, for a community, for a school, or, in our case, for a leadership group to come together as one around a common intent.

> *May all be happy,*
> *May all be without disease,*
> *May all creatures have well-being,*
> *And may none be in misery of any kind.*

As a team, consider the following questions:

❧ Who do we want to be happy, to be free of disease, to have well-being, and to be free of misery? Do we include the entire staff or team, or are some left out?

❧ If some are left out, why is this so?

❧ What steps can be taken to embrace those who are left out so they feel included?

## The Decision Tree

### *Who am I serving?*

*Humanity*

*The nation*

*The wider community*

*The immediate community*

*My family*

*Me*

# CHAPTER 6

# ON THE BUS

I T WAS FRIDAY NIGHT, AND some friends had joined us for the journey north into the English Midlands, where we were going to have a quiet weekend of contemplation, meditation, and inwardly refreshing activities. After all, we really deserved it at the end of another full-on week at school. Then – yet again! – the phone rang.

I glanced at the flashing name. This time, it was a sports master, one of several who under normal circumstances would be ensconced in the post-week review at the local watering hole. So why was he calling the head, several hours after all the boys had well and truly departed from the premises. It must mean trouble.

'Hi there. All well?' I knew it wasn't, but how else do you start such a conversation?

'Well, no, not really', he replied. There was no point in trying to hide the fact that we both knew something was up.

'I'm sorry to hear that. On a scale of one to ten, what are we dealing with?'

'A seven – but it could be an eleven!' he replied, trying his best to stay calm.

Now, calls like this can tell you as much about the caller as about the incident itself. In this case, the colleague was experienced, but obviously extremely anxious. He hadn't yet lost his composure, but could easily do so. The next couple of minutes would determine whether we had a real crisis or something else. It is always the way you greet pending disaster that matters most and sets the tone for what is to come.

'It's about Danny', he said, referring to a sixth former who perpetually kept his head down but lived a kind of shadowy existence. His parents had split and often neither of them was in the country. 'At the end of games this afternoon ...' (held at the sports grounds of a local university) '... he was caught in the shower with someone'.

I paused.

'Boy or girl?' I asked tentatively, knowing that at an all-boys school it might well have been the former, but hoping it was the latter; good old-fashioned heterosexual scandals are much easier to deal with when it comes to informing the parents. Having to 'out' a lad to his mum and dad, especially in such circumstances, is no fun at all.

'Girl', he said.

Quick as a shot I retorted, 'Thank God for that! I thought we had a real problem on our hands'.

My colleague roared with laughter; the whole sense of crisis had been removed from his mind, and he was free to think and speak of what to do next without feeling guilty and blameworthy. There was an enormous amount to do, very quickly. Danny had 'bumped into' his girlfriend, a Year 11 pupil from a local state school, on his way to games that afternoon and they had arranged a rendezvous. The chief grounds man from the university had seen her go into the boys' shower room after the other lads left (or so he thought), waited a little while and then, not seeing her come out again, went to investigate. Having discovered the youngsters in a compromising situation he proceeded to deliver a lecture worthy of the School Chaplain before phoning the sports master and asking him to take 'the strongest possible action' against the boy; otherwise, he would ask the university authorities to bar the whole school from using their facilities. Now, that would be a problem.

An immediate apology to the university was necessary, and to the grounds man. I knew I could trust my colleague completely to deal with the situation properly. The boy would have to be dealt with, but that could wait until Monday, as could a call to the girl's school and most other required actions. Together we would have to repair the reputation of the school and it would be rather nice to keep it out of the local papers. They loved such stories, especially involving a school and a boy who meditates (why that would make a difference, I don't know). We would have to keep this as quiet as we could. I could trust my colleague to manage the local gossip at the university and amongst the sports teachers from several other schools that also used the grounds.

'I agree with you, boss', he told me. 'Have a good weekend!' ... which we certainly did. My trust in him allowed that to happen.

Having the right colleagues on your bus, as Jim Collins describes it, as you journey to fulfil your intent is essential to success in any enterprise. In a school, it is rather more difficult to achieve without an enormous dose of patience, unless you want to take on the unions, your governors, and half the staffroom, all at the same time. Patience in getting the right people on the bus, along with having a heart and mind open to the idea that even the hardest of eggs might crack one day, are the magical ingredients.

Every new head will want to bring change, and in most situations, change is both desirable and needed. But what is meant by change?

Change is not just a new way of doing things or a different set of objectives; change lies in attitude and intent. Until that is realised, the way things happen will not change. Failure to recognise this is why the vast majority of 'change campaigns' in enterprises fail.

When I arrived at St James to assume the headship, the attitude of the vast majority of staff was understandably negative and anxious. Many of the older hands had felt passed over, not just for the headship, but for promotion of any kind. They had devoted themselves to an educational ideal, an exciting new initiative, thirty years earlier, but in recent years had been treading water. There had been virtually no professional development and certainly no managerial organisation or opportunity for acquiring new skills. What they had was an enormous understanding of the principles of the educational experiment St James had embarked upon. In this they were 'world leaders', although when this was mentioned to some of them, they modestly denied it all. They preferred to see themselves as 'just teachers'.

A small number of younger, more recently employed members of staff saw the new head as their chance to shine and move ahead. They wanted things done differently and were prepared to work to win his trust and favour. They had a sense that their new boss might make a managerial change and that they might be given fresh opportunities; after all, he knew nothing about running schools.

All management textbooks tell you not to overcomplicate structures; not to have too many people involved in decision-taking; not to promote people without clearly knowing that they can do the job. All of this sounds right enough in theory and makes a sort of common sense, except that as with all textbook advice, it does not take account of the extraordinary and the practical. This was an extraordinary situation and it needed a practical solution. The only team to play with is the one you have.

Two things were clear. First, it is a waste of resources not to harness experience. Ageism is a subtle crime and is one reason why our society is so unbalanced. A man or woman with an older body may not be able to move so fast, but his or her mind has a depth just from having seen and done many things over a longer period of time. People with experience need to be used, both for their sakes and the sake of the enterprise. Second, it is equally wasteful, and a very short-sighted perspective, not to harness the vitality of youth, but to do so requires trust and confidence. Younger colleagues must be put into responsible positions in the sure knowledge that they *will* get things wrong and mistakes *will* be made. That is inevitable, like night following day. My own experience has shown, however, that even when mistakes are made, they are usually not too serious and, with a touch of wisdom, they are easily repaired; equilibrium is restored and the experience gained is extremely useful.

But would the 'old' and the 'young' want to work together, or would they end up frustrating the living daylights out of each other? I thought, based on my then six months in post, that they probably would scrap and snipe, so I decided on an unconventional approach. Two leadership groups were formed: one, the Heads Advisory Group, peopled by the older more experienced players; the other, a youngsters group composed of the next generation of leaders, who I called the Senior Management Team. The SMT's remit was to do things the best way possible and if that meant changing everything, they should go ahead and try it. The HAG was to set the strategic course for the next few years; it should look at things like curriculum and timetables, the admissions policy, marketing, and how our brand of education could be modernised without forfeiting its essence.

Key to making these two groups happen was one young man, a teacher of modern foreign languages, who at that stage was not even a departmental head. He clearly had the ear of the young staff members. And having had an 'emotional contract' conversation with him at the start, I knew he wanted management responsibility. It was equally clear he was up to it. So I appointed him Chairman of the SMT and asked him also to sit on the HAG. His job was to tell the HAG what the SMT were up to and, even more importantly, to tell them how the younger staff members felt about things. He was wise enough to know just how far to push the boat out without offending the HAG and clever enough to communicate to the SMT that their points were getting across.

The other key to making a success of this less than conventional approach was the decision to tell members of both the HAG and the SMT that they were only in post for two years; that at the end of that period, the whole process would be reviewed and might well be changed; and that I needed time to see how they worked together and whether individuals were suited to the jobs they had been given. I knew this was a dangerous proposition as any one individual, at the end of the period, could object to a change in function, and could use the burgeoning UK employment laws to assist him. But it was less risky than putting the wrong person in the wrong seat, even if he was on the right bus. The governors seemed to accept the approach, based on their lack of objection rather than any strong affirmation.

At the beginning the whole experience was very bumpy, a simple fact that I pretended to ignore. When everyone thinks you know absolutely nothing about what is going on, you have a certain advantage. You can blithely pass over things and let them unfold in their own way, knowing that time will tell. The key to this approach, however, is staying absolutely wide awake and watching everything. Most people are consumed by events, rather than by the fact that you, as head, are watching both the events and them. This provides you with quite an advantage, at least for a while. It also saves acres of energy.

Giving time for something to settle down so you can see what is likely to be the outcome is a seldom employed leadership technique, usually because a related interest group or constituency is demanding immediate results. Schools, by their nature, tend not to be like that; however, our few inset days each year were vital if change was to happen at St James.

By the end of the first term of this new leadership arrangement, one or two green shoots of hope had appeared. The team of youngsters was beginning to stage school events with a new level of professionalism. They were sorting out the vexed issue of 'cover work'. They were taking the sting out of complaints from colleagues by not just listening to them, but acting. They were feeding back to the HAG and they were winning acceptance for their ideas to change our ways of working. They were leading brilliantly.

By the end of the first year, not one major decision made by the new, dynamic SMT had been overturned by the HAG. This was as much a testament to the HAG's willingness to buy into the new approach as to the SMT's ability to get things done, and done well.

The HAG had become much more of a reflective talking shop, which was exactly what had been hoped for. Issues that had not been looked at for years were coming into view, and the wisdom of years of experience was being directed towards solving the numerous problems.

The approach was not quite nirvana. Not everyone who had an opinion was asked to join the HAG, so the grumbles corner in the staffroom often vibrated with discontent during break-times. The calculation was that this was far less damaging to morale, especially of the younger staff members, than having numerous staff meetings to consult on either strategic or organisational issues. The hope was that the HAG would fight their corner when in the staffroom, which only partly happened. As the temperature rose, the HAG began to feel the heat of leadership, something most had previously not experienced.

Observing what was happening whilst trying not to become depressed by the vigorous criticism that emerged on a regular basis did give a fresh view as to what the people dynamics in the staffroom were (see chapter 8) and whether the team I wanted on my bus was anywhere near forming. Some rather timely retirements created space, as did a couple of helpful resignations. A healthy turnover of staff keeps every enterprise fresh, though this was a novel view for many at the school. By the end of year two, there were several empty seats on the leadership bus that needed filling and a number of new internal candidates wanting to fill them.

By this time, the HAG was also showing its vulnerability. No one could doubt the enthusiasm for the new approach, but some key players were struggling in their individual roles, simply because they had not received any formal training. This was a failure on my part, which I justified at the time by saying there was just too much else to do: if people couldn't do the job to the professional level I required after two years of trying, they would have to step aside.

My political and business experience had left me doubtless that moving people out of the HAG seats would create new difficulties, especially as they were valued members of staff as teachers and they had been loyal to the school for years. One rather astute member kept reminding me of how much social contact he had with the Chairman of Governors! Adding to the pressure were the SMT: they wanted much more of a say in strategic development and were frustrated by not being able to sink their teeth into the meaty issues. If you create a tiger in your management structure, you have to be prepared for it to bite when it feels confident enough. And they were certainly biting now.

Getting the right people onto the bus and having them sit in the right seats is only part of the issue; shaping the structure of the bus in such a way that it is not top-heavy is also important.

Whilst it seemed absolutely right to abandon the HAG concept as a whole at this stage, it did not seem right to abandon the people. Some of them might not be right for the executive roles they had been asked to play, but they still had good opinions and interesting views that should be harnessed in some way.

Instead of trying to change these people to fit into pre-defined and regularised roles, I tried to look afresh at their strengths and create roles ideally suited for them. Whether they were part of a formal management structure was not as important as finding roles that would bring real satisfaction to the individuals. One had a roar like that of a lion but was as gentle and caring a soul as you would wish for; he was ideal for overseeing school discipline, where we needed a balance of firmness and love. Another struggled with the administrative efficiency now being demanded by 'the young Turks', as I called them, but he had a real essential understanding of the importance of boys learning the actual knowledge in a subject. He stepped from one executive role into another one, less demanding and modified to be more suitable to him. The policy of always finding a round peg to fit a round hole does not work in practice: you have to change the shape of the hole if you want your more experienced people to be useful in your school.

Several of the former SMT, whose average age was in the mid-30s, were invited to stay on the team. This became the only leadership group managing both strategy and organisational development. A new group, formed of even newer and younger staff members, were invited to manage events in the school calendar: speech day, church services, sports day, etc. This would be an excellent training opportunity and provide hands-on professional leadership development, something so lacking up until then.

The governors also came into play. Because the numbers of pupils were growing in the three schools they oversaw, newly formed governors' committees needed to be created, one for each of the London schools. I seized on the opportunity to put staff members no longer on the HAG into that group. Now they could operate at the highest level, have an ultimate sanction on direction of the school if needed, and certainly maintain their respect among their colleagues. My regret now is that I did not give them sufficient help in understanding how to 'play' their role on a committee like this. They saw the committee only as a sinecure for having been removed from the HAG, which is a shame.

Despite the difficulties and imperfections – and there will always be such hiccups when constructing a leadership team – the bus was now powered up with all the seats adequately filled and a number of brilliant, keen, and dedicated young leaders ready to roar. They had two years to get the school into shape for an inspection.

When the call eventually came from the Independent Schools Inspectorate saying that we were to be visited, I was confident we were in good shape. I wasn't around to take the call; my new young deputy, who had previously been Chairman of the SMT, took it, dealt with the transmission of mountains of material, and lined up a schedule for the inspectors. He and the new SMT continued to manage the process excellently, having attended several training sessions on effective inspections, each of which emphasised how important it was for the head to step back and let those who really know their roles get on with the job!

Deciding who should be on the bus is one of the key decisions faced by the head, especially when first arriving at a school. The debate as to the best method of choosing a leadership team remains contentious, mainly because many of the processes are so theoretical and the acknowledged experts cannot agree. There are numerous personality tests on offer by teams of highly proficient authorities. Frankly, most only confirm what you already know; their value is that they give you a language with which to communicate to certain team members why others on the team are acting in a particular way.

We have already examined the emotional contract of team members (see chapter 2), which by virtue of its ability to involve the whole team in a process of self-discovery has an added advantage of serving as a team-building process. Experience has also taught that one other critical factor requires consideration when pulling the team together. It is what Eastern philosophers call 'the balance of the energies'.

This concept of the energies is central to much of the East's understanding of how things happen. The idea is that the world turns on three dynamic forces (called *gunas* in Sanskrit); that by extension, all three underlie human existence; and that a unique balance of these energies is built into each individual's nature. To further this idea, the tradition teaches that over time, by undertaking various practices or behaving in certain ways, the balance of the energies can change.

The first energy is soft and reflective. It is the energy that allows someone to see things clearly, both in his own mind and the world around them. This *sattva* force is rather swan-like; a person with lots of it can move around untouched and unfazed by events, yet knowing exactly how to respond to them. This kind of power is accumulated by the regular practice of meditation or silent reflection. If you have ever got up early and looked out to sea just as the sun is rising, or sat on a mountainside looking towards the horizon as the sun is setting, you will have tasted *sattva*. When it is present, it is impossible to be anything other than blissful. This is one reason why the sages of old always recommended that their disciples meditate at sunrise and sunset.

The second energy is vigorous; it is the energy of activity and movement, known as 'rajas' or tiger-force. Without this energy, nothing would get done. Some people can never stop doing things; such characters are full of *rajas*. If they don't have enough *sattva* in their constitution, their *rajas* force will them keep turning . *Rajas* propels people to and from work every day, around their offices, schools, or places of business, and throughout most of the waking hours. It is the force behind the 'rush hour' (a wonderful term to describe humanity's mass movement). When *rajas* is predominant, it is not the time to be meditating!

The consequence of a day of *rajas* is inevitable: the energy called *tamas* – the dull, sleepy, or sloth-like energy – naturally arises. This is the energy of physical rest and recovery, the force that prevails every night when we sleep deeply, but also which sneaks in after lunch on Sundays and doesn't allow us to move from the comfort of our living rooms. It makes us heavy and lethargic.

For health and well-being, a balance of the three *guna*s is needed, but at any one time, two of them will be more active and the third will lie low, ready and waiting to arise when its time comes. These energies show not only in the physical body; they also influence our states of mind.

When conducting a meeting, a head will need a good measure of *rajas* to keep things alive, but he will also need to ensure a sufficient measure of *sattva* so that the participants can hear what is being said and understand it. If the team or staff are full of *tamas*, then it's better to save your breath until they wake up. When a big decision needs to be taken, it is best if the mind is still and full of *sattva*, to allow the various matters to be carefully inwardly reflected upon, without the rush of other thoughts and anxieties.

Most resistance to change is because of a prevalence of *tamas*, the force of inertia. One of the greatest challenges is to find ways to shift that inertia; unfortunately, there is no magical ingredient. Once again, a patient and persistent approach is necessary.

Another way to understand these energies is to see them as 'atmospheres'. The atmosphere of *sattva* is exceptionally light and harmonious, full of simple happiness and co-operation. The atmosphere of *rajas* is one of precision and effectiveness; it makes the whole room reverberate with sharpness and brilliance, along with creativity and the sense that things are really happening. The atmosphere of *tamas*, other than in the dead of night when it is properly placed, is one of heaviness and tiredness, where nothing is happening, no one wants to contribute, and everything feels flat and unproductive. (How many meetings have we conducted or attended that were filled with this energy?)

Very few people are naturally full of *sattva*, but every leader needs some of this energy; otherwise, he will simply lose focus and direction. Many more leaders are full of *rajas* (especially deputy heads), and thank goodness for that too. Schools are remarkably active places, but without sufficient measures of *sattva*, all the *rajas*, which creates the activity, could easily be poorly directed. *Tamas* is natural to every human being so you need not look too hard to find it.

The ideal team on the leadership bus is a collection of characters who, between them, are able to be efficiently reflective and active. If the whole team are brilliant doers but there is no one who can step back, remain detached, and provide a check on direction and progress, trouble will not be far away. Unfortunately, even the wise say that defining someone's energy balance is not a precise science, not least of all because the energies are changing all the time. Starting to look for which energies are at play and observing colleagues from the perspective of their energy balance is, however, remarkably revealing. Over the course of a term, you will get a sense of which atmosphere they exude at work and what their natural inclination is. If the balance of energies on the bus is either not active enough or not reflective enough, then change is a must.

The balance of forces in the leadership team will also determine how fast the bus is travelling, as well as its direction. Here, a number of points should be noted.

First, speed for its own sake is not always a good thing. We are virtually programmed to think 'fast is good', whereas in reality it may be reckless. There is also a world of difference between *sattva*-slow and *tamas*-slow; the first is a careful, considerate, and happy journey towards change whereas the latter is simple inertia. To glide slowly with grace like a swan is a very different experience to lagging lethargically like a sloth.

Over recent years, a 'slow movement' has emerged in society, proposing the benefits, for example, of cooking food slowly and walking slowly; everything is done with mindfulness. This is *sattva-slow*. I believe it provides a lesson for headship too. Constructing a leadership team where there is sufficient willingness to proceed with change gently and reflectively yet purposefully is an ideal to be aimed at.

Such an approach will enable a firm foundation to be laid in any organisation, which, when it is inherited by the incumbent leader, can be built on, not destroyed, by his uncontrolled *rajas*. This is another dimension of the Jim Collins Level 5 leaders: they leave a legacy from which even greater things can unfold. The driver of the bus may change, and so too may the occupants of the key seats, but there is no need for the bus to alter direction. School leadership, as the great head teachers and their great schools can testify, is a long, slow, *sattva*-filled vocation.

## Inner Disciplines to Help Balance the Energies

For any individual to get the energies into balance, a number of lifestyle choices should be made. Some of the key activities would involve the following:

1. Spend fifteen or twenty minutes every day in some form of reflective activity. Meditation, breathing exercises, walking meditation, yoga, or Pilates are some suggestions (see chapter 11). Mindfulness exercises of any kind will slowly change the balance of mental and emotional energies, creating more *sattva*.

2. Eat mindfully and slowly. Most of us rush what we eat and, as a consequence, barely taste our food or know when to stop eating. Over-eating and drinking produce *tamas*; not leaving enough space in our stomach for digestion equally produces *tamas*. Slow, mindful eating, however, allows the inner Knower to tell us when to stop and also what the body needs. Certain foods create more *sattva*, *rajas*, or *tamas*. Meat products, especially red meats, are *tamas*-producing; a vegetarian diet is more productive of *sattva*. Hot spicy foods result in *rajas*. Drinking ice-cold drinks with a meal puts out the digestive fire, leaving food products in the stomach and bodily channels for too long, creating heaviness and *tamas*. Meat can take days to digest; vegetables turn to energy in just a few hours. Just watching what we eat, and while eating, doing so mindfully, will over time alter our energy balance. Turn to books on Ayurveda (the Vedic science of health) for more detailed information on foods, body types, and the energies.

3. Sleep at times most conducive to deep, sound sleep. Just like the individual, the universe too has its rhythms and measures. The two hours before midnight and the two after midnight are the best times for natural rest and

deep sleep. At around 2.00 a.m. the subtle atmosphere changes and deep sleep (primarily *tamas*) moves into a dreaming sleep (now mixed with *rajas*). Often, there is a natural awakening in the early morning (5.00 to 6.00 a.m.), which is *sattva* time. Instead of turning over, why not get up? If you do, there will be time for meditation and reflection or gentle yoga-type exercises. After a few weeks of trying this, your body will take on a new rhythm. You will not slump in the sofa when school ends, dozing in a kind of half-haze. You will find yourself more mentally refreshed, with more *rajas* during the day, and your efficiency will improve, as will your health. Turn to books on mind-body medicine (such as those by recommended authors Deepak Chopra, Dr Sunil Joshi, Dr Andrew Weil and David Frawley) for more information.

CHAPTER 7

# CLUBBING IT

J UST AS YOU WOULD NOT expect a golfer to use a putter to drive
his ball off the tee, but rather to pick the appropriate club for
each shot, so you should not expect a leader always to use the
same leadership style in every situation. With experience, he must
have evolved a collection of styles, or clubs, which are available to
him at all times to use in different circumstances. As every ama-
teur golfer knows, it takes practice to use a club well, even when
you have chosen the right one. In the same way, knowledge based
on experience is vital in utilising leadership styles, and that only
comes with experimentation.

Dr Daniel Goleman and his associates, Dr Annie McKee and
Dr Richard Boyatzis, *(Primal Leadership: Realizing the Power of
Emotional Intelligence)* have led the way with some brilliant work
on unfolding a practical understanding of leadership styles: the
analogy of the golf bag and its clubs is entirely theirs. It's reading
I highly recommend, as young leaders can too easily sit back and
think, 'Well, this is me and this is just how I do things', without
trying to expand themselves or approach situations they must face
differently.

Understanding which leadership club to use in which circumstance does not create a leadership stereotype or clone. Every 5

iron in the golfer's bag is pretty much the same, and yet no two golfers use it identically. So the model gives plenty of scope for individuality and personality to shine. The head's nature and approach to life, with his own balance of the *sattva, rajas,* and *tamas* energies, will be evident as he uses these clubs. Depending on his nature, he will have to work harder at some swinging styles than others; he will, through experimentation with each club, find that he uses some of them quite differently from the way his colleagues use them. Understanding your own leadership 'swing' is an intensely individual matter.

A consummate utiliser of the leadership clubs in mid-1980s political life, even before the analogy came to the fore, was former Foreign Secretary and Leader of the House of Commons, Francis Pym. Well-bred as a country gent, Francis was not the same kind of leader as his boss and prime minister. According to Goleman's classification system, his dominant leadership style would be *affiliative*; hers would be *pacesetting*.

Francis liked to let people feel that their point of view mattered to him, and he would spend time in the political arena deliberately showing that he was listening carefully. He would make the effort to let you know why he was either going to ignore what you had to say or accept at least some of it. Behind his affable exterior was a much more hardened politician than many gave him credit for, a fact which became known to those who worked with and for him when he persistently refused to accept all that you offered to him. He was definitely his own man.

It was clear to see that such 'affiliativeness' frequently drove Mrs T mad, leading her to describe him as either 'wet' or 'not one of us'. The phrase was used to describe anyone who was not hard-nosed and prepared to brush all others aside in the quest for fulfilling a vision. Goleman would describe her approach as that of a classic 'pacesetter'. The pacesetter is someone who clearly knows where he is going and what he wants, generally disregarding all those who counsel caution. To be a successful pacesetter requires a cast-iron resolve and a thick skin; Mrs T had the former, but not always the latter, as her reaction on the loss of Conservative Party leadership a few years later clearly showed.

Francis had assumed the role of the Foreign Secretary after Lord (Peter) Carrington resigned, following the loss of the Falkland Islands in 1982. Francis was in favour of a British task force being sent to the South Atlantic, but was equally in favour of an American initiative led by the US Secretary of State, Alexander Haig, to negotiate a settlement. Such a balanced response from the British diplomat is typical of a leader whose natural style is predominantly affiliative. Mrs T on the other hand wanted the Falklands back in British hands, lock, stock, and barrel, and quickly, and nothing was going to stop her getting them. If an agreement to get rid of the invading force could be negotiated, that was fine, but she was not going to put her task force, then steaming towards Falkland Sound, on hold for a single minute – a typical pacesetting response. A clash of predominant styles, not just political will, between the British War Cabinet's two leading personalities was inevitable. It was only a matter of time and circumstance before something would change.

Just a few days after Francis became the British Foreign Secretary, his US counterpart, Alexander Haig, who himself had seized the opportunity to show his own *directive* style of leadership, announced to the world that he had a deal on the table with the Argentine dictator, General Leapoldo Galteiri. The directive style is nearly always marked by certainty of purpose with a slight allowance for others to hold a different view. Accepting a compromise peace deal would stop a war, but on-going negotiations about the sovereignty of the Falklands would be required. Mrs T could never accept it; the pacesetter's vision would be undone if she did. Every bone in Francis's body wanted to agree. That was how an affiliative leader would want to work: take what is there now and push for more later.

It was a Sunday afternoon and we had all flown north to Scotland for a regional Conservative Party conference. As we arrived to prepare for Mrs T's speech, which, because of its timing, had far more political and diplomatic significance than her normal party polemics, we found Haig wanting a response to his peace deal. He wanted to announce that the US had brokered an end to a war before it started and that he had personally triumphed in the role of international peace-maker. A big ego often accompanies the directive leader. (Leadership observers may recall how Haig assumed control of the American nation after President Regan had been shot – a directive response, but rather premature since it undid his political career.)

I found myself in the Prime Minister's hotel suite with Francis and Cecil Parkinson, the Conservative Party Chairman who had been drafted into the War Cabinet because of his abilities as a communicator on television, especially for the overseas market. The pacesetter was in no mood for compromise – none at all. The affiliator was in no mood to be bullied; he had just been given the job, and so the political fallout that would result from his resignation at this delicate time would torpedo the Prime Minister, the war effort, and the Conservative Party all at once. Both Cecil and I knew the stakes had never been higher.

The time was approaching fast when we would have to leave the hotel and go to the conference hall. The media sensed a massive story. Francis argued his case. Mrs T, doing her best to control her anger, brushed it aside, again and again. Pacesetters who believe they are totally right are absolutely unbreakable; only events themselves tend to cause them to crack, not reason and certainly never threats. Francis gently put on the table that he too felt very strongly, and that he would have few options left but to resign his post if he could not at least signal to the Americans some willingness on behalf of the British government to keep talking and negotiating. There was a very slim compromise, but enough for both politicians to live with. The Haig deal was not good enough, but the British would be prepared to negotiate a full Argentine surrender and their immediate withdrawal from the British territories they had occupied. In the meantime, the task force would keep steaming ahead into the South Atlantic.

Later, when the story of this battle of wills between the Prime Minister and the Foreign Secretary emerged, Francis found himself severely criticised by sections of the popular media for being weak. He was criticised by the Thatherite right for wanting to 'give away the Falklands' and he was criticised by his own supporters for not being more firm with Mrs T. He was deeply hurt by this. In fact, it was the affiliator in him that had found the words that allowed his pacesetter boss to keep her honour intact while maintaining the honour of British diplomacy, skills which were well-known across the world. Real affiliators are very good at this; even in the tightest spot they find a way through. But real affiliators are often vulnerable and super-sensitive. It is an allowable fault, even a positive one. That is why, in my view, the *affiliative club* is the 5-iron for all head teachers. It is the club most likely to promote harmonious progress and the one most likely to get you out of trouble. All heads should practice using this style as often as possible.

This story also shows the dangers of adopting the directive style. There are times when it is absolutely essential, but they are fewer than at first might be thought to be the case. If your school is on fire, you don't want to have an affiliative or even democratic discussion; you want good clear *directions* to leave the building as fast and as safely as possible. If something needs to happen quickly, and you are very clear on the need, then this is the appropriate club to use. If you have inherited a bag of worms when arriving at a new school and some change must happen, again this is the best style to use. In golfing terms, the directive style is your 3 iron. It looks harmless enough but is in fact very difficult to use successfully or frequently. You certainly do not want to use it when you are approaching 'the green'.

Greens on the golf course are very smooth. Most experienced heads will tell you that on their 'golf courses', there are plenty of holes waiting for them to fall into, but not many instances of gentle, unruffled calm. To aim for that, however, is always a valid goal and to help achieve this the democratic or *participative club* can be useful. This is not necessarily an easy style for a head, as many of us are rather too head-strong to use it well. If you grip this club with too much force, the shot will certainly be off mark.

Here it needs to be made clear that different clubs can be used simultaneously with different groups. You may want to be participative with your senior management team but directive or affiliative with your general staff.

To help quell the squeals of protest at change in the staffroom, accompanied by cries that 'he is not listening to us', I introduced not more formal staff meetings, but an informal process called *staff forums*. Despite having a largely open head's office door at key times of the day, I found that only certain people came through it. Something else was needed for vociferous members of staff who did not come in to voice what they were thinking to give them the sense that they were participating in school life.

The staff forum deliberately had no agenda and took place after school. To help lubricate things a glass of wine was offered and we sat in a circle. Word went out that staff from all parts of the school could come and any topic or question could be raised. At first, a handful of stalwarts came to express their obviously heartfelt issues. Some I had already considered, but I had clearly not communicated why certain things were not happening; we often forget that telling people why we are *not* doing something can be as helpful as telling them why we are. The forum allowed me to explain; the more intimate setting helped ease the dialogue and I tried to encourage (with only partial success) people to push back. The participative club is your putter; it involves gentle encouragement.

At the same time, more action was needed when working with the new SMT. I wanted them to take ownership of the 'vision' – to gain a taste of swinging the *visionary club*. What kind of school were we creating? What was our unique proposition? What steps or changes were needed to deliver this? How was all this going to happen? So we started the process of regular *away days* of the SMT, especially at the beginning of the academic year. This is common in the business world but had never before been done by the school. By working together through such questions over several days, an interesting thing happened: all SMT members felt involved, fully participative, and affiliated to everything that was going on.

The visionary, affiliative and participative clubs are a good set, and if you don't carry the whole bag, at least keep these three with you.

When examining these styles, young leaders often want to be described as visionary; and yet without the whole leadership team buying into the vision, it is unlikely to continue after the leader has moved on. The story of Mahatma Gandhi reveals just what it means to be a true visionary.

As a young, London-trained barrister, Gandhi found himself being thrown off a train in Pietermaritzburg near Durban in South Africa simply for riding in a first-class carriage, a place forbidden to anyone with a dark-coloured skin. That incident sparked a lifetime of protest, first against the late nineteenth- and early twentieth-century South African apartheid regime and later against the oppression of British colonial rule in India.

Once Gandhi had realised his vision of amending the divisive pass laws of the Jan Smuts government, he took the deal on offer and moved on. That part of his vision had been fulfilled, even if the rest of apartheid remained in place and had to wait for Nelson Mandela to grapple with. The real visionary leader never loses the vision but is always practical. He is always prepared to move on.

When he returned to his native India, a reluctant hero, he was beset by local politicians and other forces of vested interests, all wanting him to take on the British. He quickly saw that most of them were not motivated by the Vedic sense of 'all being happy', but rather, by desire for their own political advancement. He knew clearly that without finding the way to embrace the peoples of India as a whole – particularly the Muslims and Hindus – the British would never leave their country. So before he did anything else, he toured the country, travelling into the countryside, into the villages, into the towns, into the cities. He looked and he listened. In modern leadership style terms, he did not seek their participation and did not seek to affiliate with them. He was forming his vision, because vision is always dependent upon need. The vision-ary leader is the one who firstly sees the need; as a result of this, words come forth to help him form his vision and then share it.

The leader with the greatest vision is the one who can climb to the top of the decision tree (see chapter 5). The leader with the sense of how his actions will benefit the whole of humanity is naturally a visionary leader. To unfold that vision he will need to embrace others within it, and that will require him to use all of his clubs.

Some readers may wonder why I have not described Mrs T as a visionary. She clearly had a vision for Britain, which was very dif-ferent from that of her political predecessors; and some may argue that succeeding leaders, of all parties, have continued to embrace parts of that vision. But her dominant club was the pacesetter; she needed to make things happen. Gandhi, on the other hand, ad-opted the policy of following the events, but while doing so, he never lost his vision of a free India. His refusal to take advantage of the British government's vulnerability during World War II is a case in point.

Some will also argue that Gandhi failed. He certainly achieved independence for India, but he failed to secure a new united India. Partition and bloodshed marked the last days of his life, ultimately leading to his own assassination. Fifty years on, however, Muslims, Sikhs, Hindus, and Christians share modern India with relatively little difficulty. (On the other hand, their neighbours in Pakistan have enormous troubles, perhaps a long-term consequence of its creation based on the vision of separation.)

In the management of a school, instances may arise when the head has to use all the clubs mentioned so far – affiliative, paceset-ting, directive, participative, and visionary – at the same time.

When St James Senior Boys' inherited its new thirty-two-acre site, eight miles from its Twickenham base, it was clear that a fully collaborative effort was going to be needed. At the same time, we knew an Inspection was pending. Both had to happen within twelve months.

Again, two groups were established. The SMT, under the direction of my newly appointed deputy head, and a development group to manage the move, headed by myself, closely assisted by my other deputy. The development group would provide an opportunity for some younger team players and older staff grumblers to step up and play their part. But before any of this could happen, a vision had to be unfolded.

The vision stuff was easier than expected. We had an expanse of prime land to play with. We needed state-of-the-art laboratories, a new sixth form centre, a dining room capable of seating us all, sparkling classrooms, and glorious playing fields. The vision simply came from seeing the need. The question was how to get people participating and feeling that the new school was theirs and ours.

The word 'vision' involves seeing, and there is nothing more effective than seeing something. So the senior management team and a large number of staff volunteers went to see the new site. We walked down the dark, oppressive corridors of the old building and I tried to get them to envision it with light, air, sunshine, and added space all around them. 'We'll take that wall down; we'll pull out those false ceilings', I cavalierly said as we toured. By the end of the visit we had a shared vision: a spacious, light, fresh, and harmonious environment, conducive for learning and living.

Confident that the immediate teams were with the project in heart and mind, I knew it was time to involve the current parental body in the vision. So we held open days, and my colleagues, both young and old, led groups of parents around the new school. 'I want you to see what I am seeing', said one young staff guide. 'I want you to share our vision'. Hearing this was heart-warming. And it worked! All the parents signed up to support the move.

Vision is one thing, but what about detail? This is where the other styles come into play. Our most participative staff member, not then on the SMT (but later appointed to the position) took on the role of detailing the specific requirements of each teacher: desks, chairs, filing cabinets, interactive white boards, and the rest. It was a thankless and seemingly endless task, which he executed by consulting fully with his colleagues. Only when they didn't respond did he become directive.

Another colleague took the role of communicating with the architects, planners, and builders. His natural affiliative style did not allow the left hand to ignore what the right hand was up to. It also meant, in very practical terms, that the architects did not need to attend every meeting, which resulted in a huge savings on their fees.

Pacesetting on such a project was a positive danger. Brilliant ideas of what could be done with the money poured forth from several quarters, but unless we could see them being translated into practical benefits over the next few months, such as classrooms and facilities, they were sidelined.

The participative approach came to the fore when we started planning the move. Teachers would have to give up a significant part of their summer holiday, both to move out of the old premises and into the new ones. I decided that we must all work with each other until the job was done. When the staff of one department had finished packing, they would make themselves available to help other departments. None of us would go on holiday until the job of moving was finished, and we would all return to help settle in. There were a few grumbles, but ultimately there was acceptance of our being in this together as one. I allocated ten days to pack up; in the event, the team worked so well that we only needed two. Everyone was exceptionally happy at having achieved so much so quickly, together.

As ultimate leader of the moving project, I considered not taking a summer holiday. A touch of inner reflection, however, showed that without a rest I would not be much good for anything by the time the new academic year started.

Upon my return from a couple of weeks of wonderful sun and sand, the school building manager approached me, rather solemn-faced. 'I know you have been watching events through your emails while abroad, but I'm sorry to say the situation is far worse than we have been saying. We didn't want to worry you!'

I was grateful for that, but not so happy when I found out the state of the building works. Everyone knows that builders always have delays on home development projects, but three weeks from the start of the new school year, we still did not have our sixth form centre, our dining room, and several classrooms, and the common areas were a mess. At least the rugby posts were up and the flagpole was flying the St James flag! A directive style of leadership was now desperately needed.

Heads are not trained as project managers, but every head involved in building projects that I have spoken to has had to become one at some stage. When I looked at the state of things, my stomach turned; there was no way we could start the school year. 'But we have to start,' I heard myself say to myself. 'We have to find a way'.

One of the sayings Mrs T was fond of repeating to her close colleagues was 'I never think about defeat. It is an impossibility'. The same words came back to inspire me. But how to act?

Try as I might, I could not see the way forward. It is courting disaster to become directive without knowing which direction you want to take. Experience has shown that you have to keep looking and listening. So for four long days, I walked the site. I talked to everyone I could find – of course the project manager, but also the plasterers, the carpenters, the painters, the plumbers, and the electricians. They were the ones doing the work, and they were the ones with the knowledge.

Experience has taught me that becoming intensely quiet and letting the mind reflect on the knowledge available can save hours of worry and allow an efficient solution to arise. Just as I was about to ring the chairman of the Board of Governors and ask for a delay in the school opening, the mind produced a list of what had to happen, in what sequence, and what follow-on actions had to take place. An inner intelligence had worked it all out and all I had to do was write it down.

'Right, we are not going to finish the dining room . Let's stop work there, relocate the plasterers and electricians, and find a marquee. The boys will love eating in a tent!" And so it went on. The project manager, building manager, and architect were relieved. We compromised. The 'director-head' was now giving extremely clear directions, swinging the *directive club*, but not wildly.

With less than forty-eight hours before our introductory day for boys new to the school, acres of paint still had to be applied. The contractors decided to work exceptional levels of overtime and with no extra pay. As the new boys entered the school on their first day, the doors were firmly closed to the west corridor, despite the fact that classrooms for the new boys were at the far end of it. The reason was simple: the painters were still at it. The strategy was that I would keep talking to the new boys in the school chapel until I saw a signal that the painters had finished. After one long hour, it came, much to the boys' relief and mine.

'Now, I would like you to go to your new classrooms', I finally said, 'but please walk in the middle of the corridor.' I didn't need to tell them why. A few weeks later, we held a magnificent opening ceremony for parents, pupils, and friends of the school from all over the world. It was a triumph of the leadership styles! Without them being played out to the full, the whole project would have failed.

One leadership style has not yet been mentioned: the *coaching* style. This club is not to be used in the midst of a major project or crisis. It is a peacetime tool, essential to the continuous professional development of those on the leadership bus with you.

Coaching a colleague well is a professional skill; therefore, I recommend finding personal development resources so that you can employ an expert. The head can do only so much: he can have emotional contract conversations with his senior team and give advice on how to handle things from his own experience. It is important, however, that these conversations do not descend into do-this-as-I-have-done advice. That is not really coaching – it is cloning. To coach well involves understanding the young leader's mental and emotional set-up and how to develop it best. Young leaders must ultimately be coached to be themselves (see chapter 2). When selecting a professional coach for your team, always view a range of options and ensure that the coach suits the candidate, not you.

A couple of years into the new management set-up, I asked a young professional life coach to meet with three of my rising leadership stars and offered him my perspectives on their needs. I agreed not to interfere with the coaching process, and he met the young men. Thereafter, he met each of them every half-term for a couple of hours, sometimes during school time and sometimes out of school. I was never privy to the working conversations between coach and participant; after all, it was not my life that was being changed, but theirs. At the end of the process, I was given a general report. By then, I had already noticed changes occurring and started to give fresh opportunities to all three young leaders.

Headship is fundamentally a lonely existence. You are at the butt end of most criticisms and it can sometimes seem that you are living in a sea of perpetual movement and uncertainty. Engaging your own life coach can be one solution, especially if your confidence is lowered for any reason. A coach who is willing to deal with your spiritual and emotional well-being, not just your mental and physical well-being, will help the most. One who recognises that, in the game, you have to be more of yourself to be successful, not somebody else; that you have to find your own way to swing the leadership clubs; that it is your vision that matters, not his or hers – such a coach could become your most valuable assistant. After all, every great golfer has a great caddie.

## Exercising Your Leadership Clubs

### ¶ *The Affiliative Style*

Ask each member of the SMT to work with a small group of teachers (four is perfect) to win their support for a chosen project. For each group, select teachers with different kinds of experience and try to mix the personalities. The result will be co-operation and teamwork in support of the project. Ask your SMT member to report back to the whole leadership team on the experience and the lessons learned. As the affiliative club is so important for school leaders, similar exercises could be repeated when the opportunities arise.

### ¶ **The Participative Style**

Choose young leaders to manage a round-table discussion on an issue of real significance to all the teaching staff. 'How to manage the cover work' is nearly always a winner! The discussion leader should be asked to try different ways to ensure that every member in the circle participates in the conversation. The report at the end should elucidate which strategies worked and which did not. Make it clear from the beginning that there is no success or failure in this process.

### ¶ **The Visionary Style**

Ask three or four of your most trusted leadership lieutenants to craft a 'vision document' to prepare for the next school development plan. They could do this together (which means they would have to use both the affiliative and participative clubs) or they could work independently. Communicate clearly at the start that the output from this work will be purely advisory for you as head. You will receive some magical responses.

### ◖ The Directive Style

Take your SMT out on an away day and get them to build a raft or negotiate an assault course. Give each one an opportunity to exercise his or her directive style of leadership. At the end of the exercise, spend at least twice as long discussing the results as you spent doing the task itself. (Resource groups are available to organise this kind of task for you.)

### ◖ The Coaching Style

As a preliminary to employing a professional life coach to work with young leaders (or yourself), conduct a series of emotional contract conversations with your leadership team. Try to get them to see through reflection what their own strengths and weaknesses are. Consider how issues might be resolved and try to find out whether the leader's needs are more in the emotional-spiritual or the mental realm, or both. This will ultimately help you bring the most appropriate life coach into your environment.

### ◖ The Pacesetting Style

Leave it! If a pacesetter is in your midst, he will not need help to be effective – but *you* might need help to control him! My staff will testify to that.

# CHAPTER 8

# JUNGLE SURVIVAL

'So survival in this job boils down to three things', our mentor told us at the conclusion of our heads' training session. 'Expect the unexpected. Try never to take what happens personally. Don't stay around anywhere for too long!' The first piece of advice is exceptionally practical. The second is far harder to live by in practice than to understand in theory. The third is sometimes not in your hands at all.

Schools are a special kind of community, unlike any other. They have a dynamic all their own, and each part of this jungle is often specific to itself. Being wide awake and understanding the lie of the land you are dealing with is essential to move from survival to 'thrival' mode, as one head rather in-elegantly put it.

We have an established tradition in the St James community: each day begins with a short session where all the staff who are able gather for a few minutes of meditative silence and a short spiritually-inspired reading, before moving on to the practical issues of the day. Sometimes the session is seamlessly unified: the silence is so restful and regenerative, providing a wonderful platform from which the whole day can unfold. The conversation that follows, even if it is about arrangements for 10B, have a sweetness and lightness about them. Of course, there are also days when just the opposite occurs.

Observing the staffroom in detail is most informative. Certain characters sit in the same place every day. Their expressions hardly change, whether you are telling them about the death of a pupil's parent or a review of their pay by the governors. They always seem to despise you and their expression clearly shows that everything was always far better before you arrived. It is very hard not to take this personally, as the new heads' mentor advised. But the advice is excellent, and if you don't follow it, 'they' have got you and any sense of unity and ease disappears.

There are always parts of the staffroom that are an absolute clutter. Books everywhere. Old jerseys. Tennis Rackets. Biscuit wrappings and sandwich packets. You would hope they didn't live like this at home, but sometimes you are left wondering. Somehow this clutch of mess is a comfort zone; it is an area they know you will be reluctant to intrude into and it is very much 'their' space. It is important to leave it to them.

Grace appears too as, in addition to the vast majority of gentle folk who are there to do dedicated work uplifting humanity, there are also one or two very bright spots, rays of pure sunshine and happiness. They are the ones with the quick quip to lighten heavy moments; they are the ones to bring a peal or two of laughter. They are guardian angels who need your quiet and also gently spoken gratitude and support. When times are difficult, look for them and feed them opportunities to respond to. It works wonders.

When taking the headship I had no idea about staff or common rooms, but the inner Knower told me it was a place in which to tread tentatively. Initially I waited for an invitation to enter and was very pleased I did. Even now, I try not to visit there too often during the day; the staff must have some 'head-free' space in which to be themselves and let off steam. Dropping in occasionally but always unexpectedly, however, can be a very useful practice.

In most schools there is an informal communications network. Its hub is the staffroom and it is, unfortunately, often ill-informed. Yet despite this, the head has to find some way to access it, usually to correct any wrong information and sometimes to sow the seed of an idea. Your secret weapon here is your personal assistant.

A brilliant PA, one who tunes into your thinking and has done things for you even before your rather slow, befuddled mind has got around to them, is another godsend for survival. He or she can afford to be far more assertive than you as head can be, and can speak far more directly than you might ever feel comfortable doing, especially with the difficult brigade in that corner. If the head does not have a natural empathy with the PA, it will be like operating with half a limb missing, because this person is quite probably your key appointment.

For some time, I hoped the difficult brigade might somehow just go away; that I might turn up one morning and find their letters of resignation on my desk. Once or twice this happened, but discussions with other heads have shown that such characters, even if they leave, are replaced by other difficulties. It is as if there is a natural law at work: every staffroom shall have some difficult characters.

Being able to talk informally with other heads is another essential release valve for even the experienced head teacher. This is why membership of one of the several heads' societies is important. The old adage of halving a problem by sharing it is completely true, and experience has shown that my particular problems and issues are merely variations on what many others before me have had to cope with.

The other adage, that you should 'keep your friends close but your enemies closer still', has some merit to it, but I would offer an interesting twist. If, despite it all, you try to keep the vision of Oneness operating, and if you try never to lose the sense of common humanity, even when the spears and arrows are clearly aimed at you, a turnaround is possible.

One spear-thrower had clearly practised for many years aiming poisonous darts in the direction of senior management, but now the bull's-eye target was definitely the new head. She would gather younger hopefuls around her and powwow on my multiple inadequacies. I could see the smoke rising in the jungle, but I couldn't read the all the signals. I rang my friends from the Society of Heads and asked for advice. 'Have it out with her', was the general consensus. A couple of them counselled extreme caution: make sure the atmosphere is 'friendly'; make sure she realises you are not 'attacking' her; try and be as conciliatory as possible; don't give her any warning of the meeting – just hold it. I liked the advice and, making as much of an attempt to look as casual as possible, invited her into my office for a cup of tea.

'I get the sense you are not very happy with things', I said, broaching the subject.

'That's right', she retorted, clearly sensitive about being 'softened up'.

'First, I'm very sorry you're not happy', I said (and I genuinely was), 'because you are an extremely valuable soul on this team and I want you with me, not against me'.

She stopped in her tracks.

'Do you mean this?' Her question was valid enough. I saw I had paid her too little attention (probably because she was so wretchedly awkward to deal with). I think I too would have questioned the sincerity of someone saying that.

'I do realise we have not communicated very well and I do realise that I have not given you enough time. But let's try and resolve your issues in as professional a way as possible. I am not asking you to like me; I am asking you, however, to listen to my replies. We may not agree, but I think we can disagree agreeably'.

To my relief, she accepted the invitation and I decided not to react to a couple of the under-her-breath remarks made before the substance of our dialogue began. Again, it is sometimes valuable in the process of survival to have selective hearing.

'I want to know why you are not doing anything about this', she said, launching into a long list of questions, complaints, and criticisms. What had our training mentor advised? *Try not to take things personally.* I held on to that, breathed very deeply, and then began to reply, point by point, to her lengthy collection of issues.

As I did so, I remembered a piece of advice given to me by one of the most successful majors in the elite British Special Air Services. After resigning from the army, he worked for me for a short while before taking on a royal appointment. He spoke of how the special forces often used the concept of 'the people's parliament' to help resolve difficulties. The leader of the group (always having four members) would invite each specialist to put forward his best plan for the job at hand. While much of what was proposed was based on sound judgement, some of it wasn't. The element that was not clear enough or fit for the purpose would be addressed; the leader could not just ignore it and hope it would go away. If a soldier had given time and respect to the problem at your request, you as leader needed to give time and respect in return, by telling him why it was not acceptable.

In the story of the angry colleague, I had clearly not done that. This became a very important survival lesson.

Patiently in our conversation, step by step, I tried to tell her why something was not happening; why I had rejected that proposal from the staffroom; why the time was not yet right but where I saw it fitting in later. She became quieter. I ended with an apology for not having explained all of this earlier.

Later I heard that she had told the story of how she knocked the head from pillar to post and put 'the upstart' in his place. Of course, she needed to keep her own staffroom territory intact. However, in practice, she was far quieter after our meeting. She started offering some constructive advice and I became more voluble with her. It was still a strain, but much less so and the advance in staffroom harmony was worth all the effort.

In Eastern mythology, Lord Krishna gives his beleaguered friend, Prince Arjuna, advice on surviving the battles of life. He could have been speaking to a new heads' conference.

'Do not become despondent', he likely would have told the newcomers. 'Those who are trying to get you cannot touch you unless you let them. It is a matter of mind control.

'First, cultivate the spirit within you of harmlessness and, alongside that, fearlessness. Words and vile criticisms only have their effect if you accept them. It is only your ego that is being punctured. Step back and see whether there is anything valid in what is being said, and then let it all go. This is what I call "renunciation".

'Harmlessness means to see the person in front of you as no different from your self. *Yog*, or join, with their humanity and try and see things from their perspective. Remember, in essence they are no different from you. However, be fearless in holding to what you know to be right.

'When you speak to your enemy, try and speak the truth as pleasantly as you can. Avoid speaking pleasant untruths as they will get you into difficulties.'

Jesus said something similar: 'Love your enemy. Turn the other cheek. Do unto others as you would have them do unto you.' I suppose he never expected these words to be in evidence in a book like this, but they are ideals worth pursuing and they provide extremely practical advice on surviving the outer forces in the jungle of headship.

The most dangerous of all traps is self-criticism. If there are characters in the staffroom who can bite you, none is as penetrating as those small, agitated, critical voices in your own mind. These voices are the multiple echoes of the ego. 'You won't be able to do that; no one will like you if you do.' 'You didn't do that very well, did you?' 'You're getting a bit above yourself, aren't you?' 'Come on, stop being so foolish.' 'Who do you think you are – the prime minister?'

Sometimes it can feel as if there is a little commentator sitting on your shoulder, perpetually doubting your ability to get things done properly and inevitably looking back and analysing what has just happened critically. 'You made a bit of a mess of that. What a ridiculous thing to say!' 'What a brilliant opportunity missed! When are you going to stop doing that?' 'Are you really up to this?'

If you keep these voices in your mind and believe them, they will, in time, destroy your confidence. It is a matter of inner self-control not to listen to them. The best piece of advice my own philosophical mentor gave me was, *Don't look back!* When an assembly has finished, move the attention onwards to the next thing: Don't look back! When a meeting has concluded, leave the outcome where it is: Don't look back!

Sometimes when speaking of this precept, young leaders ask, 'If you don't look back, how can you learn from the mistakes you have made?'

Reflection on the past that is of the greatest value often has some distance between it and the event in question. Real reflection is also done by what I have termed the Knower or intellect, not the ego force. Such reflection is far more dispassionate and less involved than the ego allows you to be. This subtle difference needs to be understood and appreciated.

One helpful guide is this: when the ego commentator speaks in one of its multiple voices (because it always uses more than one), it is inevitably critical, divisive, and loaded with some kind of self-centred desire. When the voice of the Knower speaks, it is never critical or divisive, but is always enlightening with knowledge and guidance. There is a world of difference between the self-critical voices of the ego and the voice of the Knower or intellect, which by nature is connected with your real essence: intelligence and love.

Establishing key relationships throughout the school community is also essential for survival: with the bursar and key governors, but also heads of maintenance and catering, medical and grounds staff, and your support staff throughout the enterprise. It is certainly helpful if you like the personalities, but that would be a bonus. Establishing good working relationships provides a consistent foundation from which your plans can move forward.

Weekly meetings with the bursar, inviting his or her full participation in SMT meetings, and alerting him to any change in circumstance that is likely to impact on the school finances is bread and butter to a smooth and successful working partnership. The jam comes when the bursar starts to fight your corner for the new projects he knows you need. Some smaller schools do not employ a separate person in this function, and often ask the head to take it on. My advice is to avoid this if you possibly can. As head, you have more important and demanding responsibilities to attend (see chapter 9).

Perhaps trickiest of the multiple relationships can be the one with the governors. Nearly every head has a different relationship with the governing body, determined largely by the personalities involved – but there are some golden principles.

Firstly, make sure you, as head, are given sufficient time to put your perspective to the governing body and key individuals within it; the chairman and the person in charge of the finance committee are the essential players. Make sure you have at least some basic knowledge of balance sheets and accounting processes. I once heard of a head who woke up with a shock to find that his school was on the verge of financial ruin because he had not been savvy enough to follow the financial reports. A head puts himself at a disadvantage, particularly in discussions, if the governors know he is weak on financial comprehension or management. Take a good course on the basics of finance or, failing that, find an accountant to give you a couple of night classes in reading a balance sheet.

Heads should always ensure they are given time to speak to their written reports at governors' meetings. It is the power of the spoken word that best communicates your intent, not necessarily the written text in your report. Governors need to hear your passion with their own ears.

Do your best to avoid politics with the governors. Some people advise building a caucus of support for your case so that you can win by a majority. The trouble with such an approach is that it is inherently divisive. You may think certain people are with you, but that means, as a consequence, that others are against you. The policy of unity or Oneness is occasionally more difficult, but it is worth the effort. It requires more patience and it often means you have to bear considerable frustration, but it creates a long-lasting platform from which the whole school – and you too – can go forward. Making it clear that you are not interested in the politics of the governing body is for the benefit of all.

One early leadership mentor passed on this tip: make sure you treat like royalty those who others see as of least significance in your enterprise. At the time, I was running the press office at

Conservative Party headquarters, where we cranked out endless press releases for aspiring Cabinet ministers. These were delivered to Fleet Street daily by a couple of elderly messengers who loved what they did, and also loved the freedom they had to stop at a number of watering holes on the way to and from their delivery points. One day, a senior party official took umbrage and put a ban on pub-crawling, not an unreasonable thing in itself but hitting at the heart of the day's enjoyment for these former war veterans. That afternoon, the package containing all the press releases was thrown off Westminster Bridge into the Thames, a fact which only came to light when the River Police returned a rather sodden bundle to Central Office. All of our work for the day had been wasted because the people who some believed to be the least important in the process had not completed their task. I immediately removed the ban, and not only did normal service resume, but also the messengers would now do anything for the boss – even deliver packages without deviation when there was an urgent need.

Regular meetings with maintenance people; popping outside to speak to the grounds man; making sure a vote of thanks is given to the catering team – all these things cost very little in terms of time. They work wonders, however, in creating a unified team.

As an increasing number of the right people took a seat on the St James Senior Boys' bus (see chapter 6), the clearings in the jungle expanded. Now, something was needed to ensure that the undergrowth was not allowed to grow thick and resistant once again.

The SMT, the bursar, and I decided to allocate a significant annual budget to the staff's on-going professional development. It should be an obvious point, but it's easy to forget in the daily rush, that human beings working in an educational setting are going to want to keep learning; in fact, if we stop learning, we cannot properly teach. Continuing education and development has proven to be one of the best investments.

Every year, each member of the staff is given an opportunity to attend at least one inset day away for professional development, along with several other inset days in-house. It is costly in financial terms, as well as in terms of required cover work for the rest of the team. However, the feeling it creates – that each person is valued and is being invested in – produces an atmosphere of common growth and team bonding. Such a healthy environment means the head has to do far less slashing of overgrowth to get through the thickets. By elevating your people to new levels of expertise, jungle branches can be turned from impediments to umbrellas that give shade and support.

Part of winning staff to your side is ensuring that key colleagues know you are looking after their career development. In conversations with several of my middle management colleagues, we have discussed their career needs and how best they will be satisfied. Sometimes they can be met within the school, but frequently they require that the teacher leave to take a promotion elsewhere. One of my goals is to create as many head teachers as possible, even with the knowledge that to do this, some of my brightest sparks will have to go and shine elsewhere.

When this policy was first introduced, several older hands expressed concern at the drifting away of talent, not knowing that it was part of a wider plan. To nip that creeper in the bud, it was necessary to examine their needs too. In doing this, I saw that their real concern was the lack of attention they were receiving; they might have been a bit long in the tooth, but they were not necessarily past professional development. Lack of attention paid to others was shown, yet again, to be the root of most leadership problems.

The modern head thus needs the ability not only to handle the greater issues, but also to give personal attention to key characters, and on a frequent basis. Most staff will want you, the top person, to attend to 'me personally'; in many cases, this will not be possible, other than in passing. It is therefore necessary to train your immediate team of leaders to give their 'direct reports' the right level of personal attention.

Leadership and management books argue how many direct reports a manager can successfully manage. There is no set answer, but experience indicates that it is not less than six or more than fifteen; if the number is greater, personal care of staff often has to be delegated or is sacrificed. This is not necessarily a popular assessment, and in practice, another strategy, such as the staff forum (see chapter 7), sometimes emerges as a good compromise. It is equally true that if someone shouts rather loudly, or is beginning to storm through the jungle, you really do need to attend to that person yourself without much delay.

The Buddha taught compassion. Compassion is where the Oneness of spirit is the prevailing atmosphere and where you do your very best to treat each person with equity and give him or her what he needs. In headship, compassion often means finding a compromise.

A member of what I called my 'trouble brigade' was an outstanding teacher but a lousy manager. The difficulty was, he wanted to be given more leadership responsibility but was less keen on the extra effort it involved, especially attending numerous meetings. Week after week, I tried to follow my own advice of talking one to one with him, albeit briefly; but sadly, it was to very little avail. We were at a stand-off.

'I don't think you get it', he told me in utter frustration, just before the end of term. Something in what he said sounded different. He was clearly experiencing an inner pain that I had not connected with before. I had written him off as a trouble-maker, full of hot air and spurious opinions; the truth is, I hadn't really 'met' him, despite the frequency of our coming together.

'You know what', I said' you may just be right. I am going to go away and try and look at this whole thing afresh'.

Now, my friends will tell me I am quite stubborn; my really close friends might tell me I am hopeless at compromise. But I do love the notion of compassion and I do hate to see anyone suffering. As I reflected on this issue, it became clear that compassion often involves stepping back from and giving up your ideas; of looking again and putting yourself in another person's shoes. As I did this, a new feeling of Oneness filled my heart and I saw the man entirely differently. Yes, of course he had his difficulties, but frankly, so did I when it came to looking after him. I couldn't give him what he wanted, because that would not serve him; but I could do something else for him, which would serve everyone else too. I hastily called another meeting.

'I want you to come with me to a special conference,' I told him. 'It is in the holidays but it will reinvigorate you. I want my senior and best people with me and you deserve a place there.'

It was a small step of compromise, but both he and I felt good about it. At the conference, we gave each other plenty of space but met up frequently to compare notes and findings. It was clear he was not only enjoying himself, but was working hard too. The compromise and compassion was working. Unity was being restored.

The sense of Oneness is an inner feeling; if it is there, it will manifest in all your actions. When there is division around you – and the jungle undergrowth creeps in on all you do – there is the need to go back and check just how compassionate and compromising you have really been. Giving people what they need, which is not the same as giving them what they want, will always be crucial to success in leadership. It will often involve compromise and the letting go, or renunciation as Krishna put it, of fixed ideas. What a relief that is too!

I find the sense that I may not be doing enough for colleagues, or not meeting their needs as much as they deserve, still comes at times, especially on Friday afternoons, at the end of an arduous week, when they have all gone home and the atmosphere becomes heavy and laborious. I am still learning not to take the whisperings so seriously, to get enough rest and recovery (see chapter 11), and then to spend some time reflecting (see exercises below) on what to do next, with as much detachment as possible from immediate events. This process always results in a fresh resolve to do better. I hope it continues to do so.

Throughout my varied career, one thing has consistently struck me. Outstanding people, whether they are politicians, media personalities, or teachers in the classroom, are prone never to feel totally satisfied with their accomplishments. This equally applies to heads. The great head is always looking to improve, always hoping to do things better, always worrying about his colleagues, his pupils, and the whole school community.

Those of my colleagues, however, who I would deem to be at the top of their game, have an inner resolve that is indefatigable. They can cope with the sniping voices, whether from the staffroom or from inside their own head. They know the direction in which to move, even if they have to make compromises to stay on track. It is not that they are impervious to the jungle drums beating around them. It is rather more that, having reflected, they have taken a stand. 'This is right. I know it. I am going forward'.

The final advice on surviving the jungle is, therefore, to be prepared to stand your ground.

Listen carefully to the feedback around you. Reflect, as detachedly as you can. Pay attention to your key people, and make sure everyone else is being paid his or her due attention. But above all else, stick to your course.

When the day comes to move on, says the third piece of advice from our training mentor, the head who has followed these precepts will know that he has, above all else, been true to himself. He will have used his innate intelligence to cut the path through the jungle. He may have upset some people along the way, but he will have achieved his vision and lived out his intent. That will bring him great inner satisfaction.

## Reflections to Help Survive the Jungle

❦ Take a little time, perhaps during the holidays at the end of each term, to reflect on some important questions: Which member of the staff requires my personal attention when school resumes? Who needs a word of encouragement? Who needs a conversation about career development? At the same time, reflect on whether your immediate reports are doing the same with their team. If there is any doubt, follow it up. Giving attention to key people at regular intervals is an important strategy for surviving the jungle.

❦ Again, towards the end of a good holiday, take yourself to a quiet place, sit down, be still, and try to hear the voices in your head. Are they critical and divisive and full of unsatisfied desire? What do they sound like? The practice is a simple one: deliberately bring to your mind a major issue at school or some of the important personalities there, and just watch as the mind 'rolls' over them. Now listen detachedly to the voices. This is putting the Knower or Witness in place. The aim of the exercise is for you to get familiar with the sound of the ego-voices so they do not seem so real when you return to daily school activity. Know that these voices are not the ones to be followed.

❦ At least once a year, give yourself some time to reflect on your key professional relationships. Are they working the way you want them to? If not, why not? What initiative do you need to take to get them back on track? (This will likely involve one-to-one discussion.) Make a note of your reflections and act on them when you return to school. Failure to do this at least annually could allow trouble to brew before you realise it has started.

¶  Reflect on where compromise is needed, either with specific people or on particular issues. How can you bring about harmony without losing your standing in the foundation of your ideas? How can you compromise but remain true to yourself at the same time?

# CHAPTER 9

# THE BEST BIT

WITHOUT DOUBT, THERE IS A crisis in headship in the UK. In the state sector, thousands of schools are operating with 'acting' heads or are actively seeking permanent replacements for those who are there. In the independent sector, the number of vacancies is smaller but the ability to attract the right calibre of head – one who really understands what independence means and how to use it – remains problematic.

Unions and heads societies will agree that the role over recent years has become loaded with bureaucracy, and despite changes to government, not much has happened to relieve the burden in practice. In the first decade of the new millennium, regulatory requirements for schools across Britain exploded, with a threefold increase in some sectors. Heads and governors were told that failure to abide by some of the most intricate regulations would result in the harshest of penalties, including the closing of schools or, where there were issues of health and safety, imprisonment. Heads had their necks on the chopping block, and not surprisingly, several prospective candidates decided it was not worth the risk.

Those who weren't deterred from taking on the role, however, did alter their work practices, in many cases quite significantly. They spent more time in their offices. They spent more money on lawyers. Most significant of all, many stopped teaching; if not completely, then very nearly so.

The inspiration that brought most heads into education in the first place – to work with pupils and their detailed care – has been stealthily taken away from them. Nobody said they couldn't teach as much, but regulators, inspectors, and governors inadvertently responded to the accelerated regulatory environment by retreating behind paperwork and, as a result, taking the very best bit of headship (the foundation of teaching our children) away from the head.

As a group of schools in the independent sector, St James has had no one dictating to them what to do; thus, its practice has been that the head teaches – a lot! Every class, nearly once a week. Mostly we teach our philosophy courses, rather than taking examination classes. The aim is to meet with every pupil in the classroom setting on a regular basis.

'This is madness', one inspector told a senior colleague during a visit. 'How can he manage the paperwork?' The answer can be found in the attitude to the job as a whole: pupils first, paperwork second. Of course, there are provisions that allow this. None of the St James schools is excessively large; and despite waiting lists, each one will remain of a size that enables the head to continue to teach for a good part of the week. It is a principle.

In a survey, the boys were asked what they thought of their headmaster teaching them regularly in the classroom, as well as meeting them in an assembly or just strolling along a corridor.

'We can really get to know him', some said.

'In a classroom, he is much closer to us than when we see him in assembly. He's really human', another declared. I breathed a sigh of relief.

'Our school has a philosophy and we can question him about it. It gets really interesting', yet another boy wrote. Our aim in these sessions is to enter into dialogue and explore some of the greatest ideas from East and West.

'He tells great stories and he doesn't make us do proper classwork like the other teachers!' Many shared this sentiment. The survey showed the pupils liked the different approach to academic lessons and they enjoyed the intimacy of the classroom.

Meeting each pupil every week gives the head a chance to see first-hand what they are like in class, as well as what kind of impression their other teachers are making on them. Being in the classroom is being on the pupils' turf, and they behave accordingly. They will also tell you things in a classroom setting that they might never say sitting in front of your imposing desk in the office.

When you do your 'walkabouts', perhaps as part of a teacher appraisal or just to watch what is happening in the classrooms, the pupils you have taught are very much at ease with you and they act naturally. They are used to being with you in the classroom setting.

On one such walkabout, I took a seat at the back of the class but with a very good side view of the rows of boys, who were trying to be inspired by a pre-GCSE *(General Certificate of Secondary Education)* grammar lesson. I noticed a slip of paper being passed along the row I was sitting in. I resisted the temptation to say something or alert the somewhat old-in-the-tooth teacher as to what was happening. It quickly became clear the message was for me.

'Good to see you, Sir', the note began rather cheekily. It got worse. 'Do you want us to wake you up before the bell?' The implication was clear: this teacher, as experienced as he was, was having trouble inspiring them. The more important message, however, was that they were comfortable with me in their classroom. I don't think I ever would have discovered how the boys felt had the relationship between us not been one of such ease.

When it comes to reading teachers' reports, your experience with the pupils enables you to look at what has been written about them with a highly informed eye. After all, you know them well. The report becomes as much about the teacher who is writing it as it is about the pupil. Dedicating time to the classroom – actually teaching the pupils your colleagues deal with every day – gives you as head a remarkable insider's view.

Of course, the best reason for getting back into the classroom has to be the sheer enjoyment of teaching and the opportunity it gives you to evolve your philosophy of education.

'What? A head should develop his own philosophy of education?' one new head exclaimed when I made this point as a guest speaker at a teachers' conference. The very suggestion that the leading teacher in a school, the head, should not just go along with what he has inherited, but rather, should use his authoritative position to evolve a pedagogy of his own was a revelation. 'Do you mean I've got the freedom to do this?' he queried further.

'Yes', I said, 'even if you are in the state sector. You may be told what to teach by the government, but not how to teach. At least not so far'.

The head is the 'leading teacher', not just the top administrator, and until the government creates a situation in which school heads feel confident teaching large numbers of pupils in the classroom on a regular basis, the change in the quality of education sought by experts and politicians alike will not come. I fully concur that in this area I may be at a disadvantage: I have not been trained as a teacher, and it probably shows in my style and approach in the classroom. Yet I see how the younger teachers look towards my example, especially when they come into the classroom with me.

There is, in fact, a considerable freedom available to head teachers, if only they will grasp it. If they do so, I believe they will find a new dimension of satisfaction in the job because they will be fully engaged in the education process, something crucial not only to student growth, but also to human evolution itself. They will be able to pass on to their younger colleagues the message that they are actually making a difference, and they will be at one with their colleagues in doing so. The 'he doesn't understand us because he is not in the classroom' rumblings from the staff room will no longer apply.

Much of the current disillusionment with headship is because too many in the role do not see themselves as making a difference. They see themselves as administrators and watchdogs for the regulators. This gives the minimum satisfaction.

Over recent decades, teachers have lost much of their social status. With such changes, it is never one event that has brought about the downfall; it is a combination of several factors over a long time. It would be so useful if a way were found for the previous elevated standing of teachers to return. A significant part in this revival could be played by heads.

Today, teachers who in the past were seen as having a spiritual leadership role in the community are no longer recognised as such. The moral example they give to youngsters is not considered as important as the so-called knowledge they offer from their rather limited university degree studies and postgraduate year of learning how to teach. While much of that year is valuably spent in classroom settings, too little of it is spent examining the psyche of the human condition and the influences that allow one society to grow and another to decline; in other words, too little of it is dedicated to examining what 'education' really is.

In my view, it is the head's role to put this back into schools. We have to take the lead with our staffs and not leave this to the PGCE trainers. The new 'teaching schools' initiative gives some scope for hope, so long as the heads and the trainers are prepared to move away from just dealing with how interactive white boards can help a child attend, and look instead at the 'being' of the child and what he needs.

The Platonic perspective on education is based on the notion of *educare:* the bringing out of that which is inherently present in the child. Every child is full of love, every child loves beauty, and every child has an innate intelligence just waiting to be unfolded.

At St James I tell the boys, 'You are pure, perfect, and free. Your spirit is eternal'. The younger ones inwardly know that is true, though they don't understand it. The older ones think about it, enter into dialogue on it, and start to question what it means to be a human being. Fortunately, there are no formal public exams on this; success lies in how they grow and develop as wholesome citizens, ready to serve the society in which they are living.

I repeat to my colleagues as regularly as possible, 'The state of your being today will communicate itself to your pupils, well before they hear from you about the latest scientific discovery or whether verbs really do operate in sentences that way. The state of your being tomorrow will have the same powerful influence. What is the state of your being? And what are you doing about it?'

I do not expect my teachers to have conquered every vice or to allow only the purest of thoughts to cross their minds, but I do encourage them to work on the level of their own being, to pursue in whatever way is natural to them a sense of self-discovery, and to keep learning and growing. I do expect them to behave the way they would expect their pupils to behave. If they follow that simple direction, every pupil will be nourished, and the teachers will have a direct connection with each of them. Yet if the teacher only gives, without regularly taking time for deep inner refreshment and re-vitalisation, there will come a point when the source is barren and dry. Too many of our young teachers are allowed to become dry too quickly.

For the past thirty-five years, teachers of junior pupils in the St James schools have dedicated the first week of their annual holi-days to going to the well for refreshment. They go away together, spend some valuable quiet time together, study great philosophic and educational treatises together, and then dedicate time to their own areas of specialization. It is a deeply nourishing time and the best use of the 'holy day' atmosphere you could wish for. Senior school teachers have more demands on their time, being burdened with such things as public sector examination requirements, and so with them we have to do things a bit differently. Every one of our inset day programmes starts with a spiritual nourishing of the human being. This is not done to inculcate the ethos; it is to refresh the minds and to get everyone back to the main point of being a teacher.

The ultimate role of the teacher is simple, but certainly not simplistic. It is to work with a youngster to find out how he can meet the present moment now in its entirety. That present mo-ment is full of knowledge, full of happiness, and full of love. Yet our society today has made that moment frustratingly illusive. Our youngsters are plugged into machines and devices for hours at a time, and we wonder why they cannot give their attention when the teacher calls for it.

Youngsters are encouraged by the media, and by some of their teachers too, to consider constantly what is going to happen next, so they miss what is happening now. Our dreams of happiness and fulfilment will never be satisfied in the future, because the future is always later; the only time for satisfaction is now.

The foundation of the pedagogy we practise at St James is to work in the present moment and take time to pause, drop everything from the mind, and enjoy the now! It works in maths, history, science, and foreign languages. It is not religious, although it can be if you want it like that. Silence, stillness, and contentment, along with clarity of mind, constitute the great gift we try to offer our pupils. None of this is written in a government-inspired curriculum. But we believe it works based on experience, and we offer it with enthusiasm and conviction. As a head, I can say it is deeply satisfying to see the results.

Heads have a unique opportunity to shape the company that fills the minds of their young charges. The national curriculum guidelines give some scope for choice; add some creative input of your own and, as head, you help determine the quality of the content of the inner being of your pupils.

We hold the view that good material is an essential nourishing force in the life of a youngster. He can learn to evolve his comprehension skills from Arsene Wenger's weekly programme notes at Arsenal Football Club; or he can do so by studying how Socrates explains the powers of government in *The Republic* or how Rumi delicately reveals the importance of love in the care of a society. Whatever goes in will have its effect, and the quality of what goes in will produce a different quality of human response.

We believe history should be taught by bringing to life the stories of our greatest men and women, and we think learning things by heart still has an important place in the school setting. One of our bright and dynamic young teachers writes plays for our youngest boys about great personalities in the growth of civilisation, magically blending the learning of history with geography, English literature, and philosophy. Her plays are creative masterpieces, and the boys love learning acres of lines – a brilliant preparation for when they perform Shakespeare's plays at age thirteen. Our annual music and speech competitions are highlights of the year, yet we don't allow the boys to enter only the 'light' or 'modern' sections; they have to be able to sing, play, or recite from the great musical and literary classics. When later people hear them using sophisticated language in daily speech, because it best allows them to express their ideas, perceptions, and emotions, a sense of satisfaction arises, as it is clear that they are receiving the best that education can offer.

If the head is thus engaged in shaping the education he is delivering and has a clear view of the kind and quality of character he wants that education to evolve, the difference he makes through his school is significant. We all say we want our pupils to be of 'good character', but what does it mean and how is it delivered? We have in society today the most sophisticated technological equipment; and the government has invested millions in new premises and the most modern teaching aids. But how much time and attention have been given to assisting heads to help teachers evolve good character in their pupils?

Sweeping changes to the curriculum, or prescribed changes to the pedagogy of mathematics or English, are going to make only marginal differences. What will make the real difference is when heads take control of teaching the great human virtues and ensure they are embedded in their school's ethos.

There are countless ways to express these virtues, and I am not proposing a single approach; such a proposition would run counter to so many of the ideas in this book. Outlined below are simply the ways we do it at our schools. I hope that heads will find the ideas inspire their own approach.

Because of our heritage we have quite naturally embraced Plato's vision that goodness is inherent in every human being and can be brought forth *(educare)* by teaching the cardinal virtues of courage, temperance, justice, and wisdom.

Courage here means the willingness to speak what is true and then to act according to what you have said. Our whole approach to education is to give boys numerous opportunities to learn to speak in public, to speak without notes, and to speak from their hearts. Every week, we dedicate one assembly to Headmaster's Question Time, where I give the students a brief account of current political and social events and philosophical issues, and then invite them to stand, ask their questions, and give their opinions. This whole school affair is inevitably dynamic. By the time a boy has sat through this every week for several years, and participated several times of his own volition, he has enormous courage to face anything. We give fifteen-year-olds leadership training, in which they learn how to give directions to others who don't want to do things; they also receive instruction on after-dinner speaking. We call on pupils to give votes of thanks, ask questions to our numerous visiting speakers – anything to get them on their feet. When visitors meet St James boys, they often comment on how well they speak and how at ease they are with new people, two vital qualities to take away from an education. Many schools have similar activities and provide a variety of opportunities; putting it all in the context of human virtue, however, rather than just skill, is the important differentiator.

The next human virtue in our approach to education is what Plato called 'temperance' and we call 'personal mastery'. It is about self-control and overcoming personal desire, especially when someone else's need is more important than your own. People will want to discuss what all this means, but it is the practice of it that matters most. Therefore, lunchtime is organised so that a boy does not eat until he has served his neighbour; a hungry boy holding back from grabbing food is indeed a triumph of his own personal mastery. Though a simple thing, it is so important to learn sensory control in a world where our senses are being bombarded perpetually, and where the advertisers' messages are about 'getting' and 'having', rather than intelligently restraining and serving others.

The Platonic concept of 'justice' offers an interesting twist to a twenty-first century youngster. It means learning to do your duty. The reason this is outstandingly appealing to young enquiring minds is that they can see its impact in modern society: what happens when people do and don't do their duty. Justice for a teacher is when he turns up ready and prepared to impart his knowledge to his pupils; failure to do so would create an injustice for his pupils. Justice for a doctor is where he delivers advice for his patient's return to health; failure to do so would create an injustice for the patient. Virtues of this nature can run in school assemblies, PSHE lessons, religious education, or even English, history, and drama. If a young person leaves school not knowing the importance of doing his duty, his education has failed, even if he has a stack of A* grades at A level.

The culmination of the human virtues in the model we use is called 'wisdom'. Philosophers, theologians, even politicians have argued for centuries over what wisdom really is. Youngsters will have none of that, so we simply say, to begin with, that wisdom starts when you take decisions and do things for the benefit of others. I point out to every new arrival at the school that when someone does something that benefits another human being, it has a ripple effect in society, just as a small stone thrown into a pool has a ripple effect.

Wisdom is essentially practical, and its sources are many and varied. When you carefully examine the great scriptures of the world, you discover that their messages are essentially the same. Their practices will be different and each one's approach may be particular, but the ultimate direction is the same. We call that direction 'truth'. Truth is unchanging, though through the ages it has been expressed in many different ways. The boys like the idea that there is an unchanging truth, not least of all because they hear the opposite every time they turn on the television or read a newspaper.

I point out to every boy, because it is central to our philosophical ethos, that we believe there is One God, but many names exist for that One God, and that the most important thing to come to know in life is that the spirit of that One God lives in the heart of every person. In this way, every religion is true and truth lives in the heart of every human being, whether he calls himself a Christian, a Hindu, a Moslem, a Buddhist, a Jew, or a member of any other creed.

I ask the youngsters what effect they think there would be in the world if more people came to appreciate this Oneness? Most youngsters say there would be more peace in the world; that people from different backgrounds would appreciate the humanity in each other, and that there would be fewer wars and fewer crimes. The vision of this appeals to them very much, and the notion that they can contribute to the development of a more peaceful and harmonious world is exciting for them.

Now, some critics might say there is no 'empirical proof' for any of this; that this is a kind of philosophical brainwashing of young minds. My response is that young minds are currently being brainwashed by all sorts of stuff, far more harmful and far less useful to the welfare of humankind. As a society, we are allowing the whole idea that the materialistic world brings happiness to continue without challenge; we are content to let young minds become full of personal and selfish desire and then wonder why nobody, including governments, can learn to live within their means. It is time for a radical return to the teaching of human values that will unify society and bring harmony to it. In my view, the head must be in the vanguard of this.

I notice that my teaching staff are unfailingly dedicated to their subjects, and those with pastoral responsibility become dedicated to the welfare of the boys in their direct care. Whether subject-based or pastoral, they all feel the calling to care for humanity. They are responding to the vocation of teaching – they are not just in a job. But I also observe that the demands we as heads put on teachers can keep them myopically centred on just their area. It is very hard, but not impossible, to get a teacher of maths to look beyond the syllabus to see that what he does, day in and day out, is to give shape to the mind and spirit of the human beings in his classroom. He is not just filling them with algebraic or geometric solutions. He is showing them a vision of the universe in number, just as the geography teacher is showing his pupils the universe in the form of its material make-up and human dynamic.

Helping the staff to rise to the universality of what they are teaching and to connect it with the human condition around them must be a function of the head. Nobody else on a daily basis is there to do that for them: to step back and see that without engagement with the wider world and the whole of the human condition, the educational process must inevitably become sterile and limited. This is what has happened across many areas of the educational establishment, and it is down to the heads in post, and the new heads who will take on the role, to change it.

Seeing the head's role like this is a world apart from being tired and bored by the endless administrative tasks that government and other institutions impose on the position. Of course, many of those jobs do require attention, but they can be shared and spread among your team of senior colleagues. If these people are worth a seat on your bus, they must be trustworthy enough to help carry the burden.

My view is that the best bit of the head's role is the teaching itself. So find a way to share the burden and get back into the classroom. Satisfaction lies there.

## Reflections on the Role of the Head

These reflections could take place over a number of weeks or months. They could be revisited after a few academic terms. They are designed to ensure that the balance of tasks undertaken by the head includes regular engagement with the pupils and sufficient objectivity to advise and guide the teaching staff.

- **Daily activities:** Keep an 'activities diary' for two or three weeks, listing hour by hour the main tasks you have undertaken each day. At the end of the period, analyse how much engagement with the educational process has taken place and how much involvement in administration. Reflect on how beneficial changes to this balance can be brought about.

- **Educational philosophy:** What is my educational philosophy? Have you written it down somewhere? During a holiday period, take a notebook and jot down your ideal educational philosophy and pedagogical approach. Reflect on how much of this is actually happening in your school.

  Note: Presently, you may be employing a very effective approach that you have evolved and practised over a long period. The purpose of the exercise is to make it explicit. Copying a best or a successful practice from elsewhere is perfectly valid.

- **Human values:** What do I believe in and what do I want my pupils to engage with? How should human values be expressed? What parts of the school day could I get involved with to help communicate the things I passionately believe in?

  A head not engaged in this will probably be feeling burdened as an administrator or something else. This is the area where real satisfaction lies, because it allows you to make a difference in the complete education of the pupils.

❦ **Administration audit:** Working with SMT colleagues, list all the areas of administration that are needed to maintain the school and its regulatory processes. Who is naturally suited to dealing with what? Can agreement be reached to share these tasks between people on the leadership bus?

CHAPTER 10

# THE OTHER FORCE

S PARE A THOUGHT FOR ZACHAEUS, the reported teacher of Jesus
when he was a boy, especially at parent-teacher interviews.
According to the New Testament Apocrypha, one of the
best reads around but so frequently left to gather dust on book-
shelves, Joseph had several difficult meetings with Zachaeus,
especially after Jesus was accused of 'bullying'. On one occasion,
some irritating lad had upset the Son of God and, as a consequence,
had the very life force itself taken out of him. There lay this poor
chap, to all intents and purposes dead as a stone, and Zachaeus
now had the somewhat tricky task of either persuading Jesus to
breathe life back into the boy or tell the boy's parents that their beloved son was no longer of this world. Zachaeus did what we would
all do: he contacted the father of the perpetrator and hauled him in
for an urgent meeting. According to the Apocrypha, Jesus relented
and sounded his special life-giving mantra; and the boy got up feeling as refreshed as an angel after a beautiful night's sleep.

Sir Isaac Newton's parents are said to have had trouble with
their prodigy too; his teachers accused him of being 'idle and inat-
tentive'. Churchill's prep school headmaster called his parents to a
meeting to discuss how the war leader of the future was nothing
but 'wilful and rebellious'.

You can never quite tell how a youngster is going to turn out, but it is a certainty that without the support of parents or guardians, our jobs as heads and teachers will not be totally successful. The parental influence is the other primary force with which we must unite if our intent and vision of creating a humane society through education is to be realised. Without heads, schools, and teachers fully embracing the needs and sentiments of the parental body and their desire for knowledge about the growth and development of their children, we are pretty much wasting our time and an awful lot of taxpayers' money.

Every child's first teachers are his mother and father, with the maternal influence being greatest at the early stages. This is not a sexist argument; it is a matter of nature. The child emerges from his mother's body, feeds on and is nourished by the milk nature has created in her breasts, and seeks from her the warmth and comfort that nine months in the womb had previously provided. So the health and well-being of mothers in our society is absolutely paramount for the welfare of our society.

Fathers are important too, especially as the child starts to grow. Whether he knows it or not, he is a force of stability and protection. One of the most frequently heard statements made by pupils in a boys school is how they want to spend more time with their fathers, how they are proud of them, or, when they are absent, how deeply they miss them.

One of the least useful effects of the late twentieth century feminist movement has been the downgrading of the role of the male in the family setting. It was brought home to me when a Dutch woman in her early thirties found she could not have children and came to ask me whether there was anything philosophically or psychologically that could be done to help her. Catching my breath from the question, I decided to ask a bit more about her personal circumstances. She happily told me she was not married and did not have a regular male partner. She didn't think she needed one as the local sperm bank was readily accessible to her. I tried to indicate to her that there were perhaps more pleasurable pursuits to help her overcome the problem and that to have a man in her life, and a father available to her child, would be an important ingredient in the development of a fully rounded human being. She refused to accept the point and left muttering obscenities about misogynists.

Multi-parenting doesn't make the role of parenting any easier, nor does it make dealing with parents any easier for the school. Just under half of the boys in my school do not live with both their natural parents. Some have stepmothers or stepfathers, and many spend the week moving between two households, often meeting two sets of half-brothers and sisters. Fewer, but still a considerable number, live with their single mother; in a couple of instances, the courts have awarded care of the children to their single father. These kinds of arrangements generally create emotional tension for the children, who are inevitably caught in the middle.

Eastern wisdom has stated for millennia that the evolution of human values and the creation of a civilised society require a child to be in the company of a mother, a father, and a teacher. At different stages of the child's development, these forces need to play smaller or larger parts; but the wisdom shows that each child should know who those forces are and what they offer, and the child should be able to turn to any one, or all, of them when he or she needs to.

The same wisdom has also unfolded guidance for parents to care for their young, and in my experience, parents love to hear of this. We may have to offer history, maths, and biology to the children, but we can also offer knowledge about the upbringing of children to their parents. Schools are becoming holistic centres for human welfare. Whether they should have to be this is debatable, but the fact is there are too few other institutions to fill the void. Traditional community fonts of wisdom, such as the parish vicar or even the local general practitioner, either are not there or do not have the time. Without schools taking on this role, the educational dynamic is incomplete and society will suffer. I have taken to giving an annual lecture to the parental body about the importance of the 'other force' – themselves – and we have followed this up with sessions on parenting from life coaches and philosophers.

The stages in human development are of the most interest to parents. There is a universality of understanding in the insights of a revered sage called Shantaananda Saraswati, who lived in northern India until his death in 1997. Shantaananda held the position of Shankara-archarya (which means teacher of Shankara's philosophy of Unity), a position of Pope-like status amongst many Hindus. Shankara himself was a ninth-century mystic who, until the age of about thirty-four, toured India and commented on the traditional Upanishadic texts. His message was of the Unity of Spirit and how the world is a play of many parts, which has to be unfolded with love and reason. The growth of a child into adulthood is one of the most important dramas going.

As with any educational philosophy or theory, the proof is only in the practice. As an educational institution, we at St James have done our best to understand his guidance and apply it in the school setting. After thirty-five years of experience, we have found that it works. When we pass it on to our parents, we ask them to try it out and not to pass judgement on it until they have experimented with it. For some, it works very well.

Shantaananda indicates four stages of human growth leading to adulthood. The first is the period from birth to five years old, which should be marked entirely as play. Everything for the youngster is a game and should be treated as such.

On hearing about this, one parent went home, and as he walked into his living room at the end of the day, heard his youngest son (age four) shout at him, 'Stop! You are about to step into the ocean where my battleships are sailing!' Usually, the father, irritated from too much stress at work and lack of sleep the night before, would brush this off. But having heard about the concept of play for the child under five, he thought, 'The whole world is simply playful,' decided to become a child himself, and entered into the enactment of his child's battle at sea. Of course, he could not resist becoming a Sea Lord, but he even found his son allowed that in the play that unfolded on the living room carpet. Later he said that from that one incident, he learnt so much, not only about his youngster, but about himself too. He decided to lighten up and take the spirit of play into his workplace, which apparently he did with great success.

Careful observation will show that youngsters of this age see very little in the world around them that is not playful. Their frustration is that the adults so frequently fail to see this too; but equally, when they do, the utter bliss that encompasses the child is tangible. I saw one father at the beach with his young son, who must have been rising three years of age, start to play catch-and-throw with a quite a small ball. The father quickly observed that his son was struggling, so instead of getting frustrated as many of us would have, he went off and found a slightly bigger ball. When the young fellow still struggled, he went off again and brought back a still bigger ball. The father had seen that the game was a growth experience for his child, but also that it was crucial to keep it as much fun as possible. So he laughed, joked, encouraged, and generally took on the persona of a slightly older boy, which his youngster adored. After the father's twenty minutes of painstaking effort, but never losing the sense of play, and by now on to the third ball, the youngster at last started to catch it and return it to the thrower. Ten minutes later, the father switched to the middle-sized ball. After another ten minutes, when his son had more confidence, the ball went down to the original size, and the youngster was catching it regularly. He was full of delight and his father was full of satisfaction. Through the idea of play, and never letting frustration set in, the father had taught his child so much. More importantly, they had bonded deeply. It was magical to watch.

The second stage is from five to ten, marked by the application of gentle discipline. Here, to help make the point, Shantaananda gives the analogy of a potter. The potter uses two hands. The outer hand keeps the shape of the pot the way the potter wants it; it is the hand of discipline. The inner hand expands the clay; it is the hand of love and expansion. To bring a child into the 'right shape', a parent (and a teacher too) must get the balance between these two hands correct. Too much inner expansion without the outer hand of discipline and the pot will not fire, or the child will not become a firm character. Equally, too much force of the inner hand and the pot will never take shape at all, or the child will be squashed. The analogy is powerful and challenging at the same time.

'But this means I will have to say no to my son', one parent responded after I had given the analogy in a lecture. 'And in his case, I may have to say no an awful lot'.

The father was right, but each child is different. In some cases, it requires saying no, and meaning it, several times. In fact, I would say from experience that it is a parent's inability to say no that causes so much difficulty in the later stages of education in the classroom. If we could help our parents to say no appropriately to their children when they are age five to ten, we would be saving ourselves and them (as well as the child) so much heartbreak later on.

Application of gentle discipline, using the two hands of the potter, should bring forth a sense of reason and responsibility in the youngster. Shantaananda does not advocate too much reasoning with a younger child: decisions work best when they are black or white. But as he approaches the age of ten, the tactic has to change.

The third stage begins at ten, marked by the child looking to expand. He suddenly starts to see things he didn't notice before, and to think of them in ways he has not considered. The whole inner world of his mind is beginning to open up and he is naturally looking for reasons for things. Between the ages of ten and sixteen the expansion of love and reason is to be encouraged. The discipline needs to be firm and, preferably, inwardly established. Good habits need to be formed, especially when it comes to school work. But wherever the word no is used, good reasons need to be given. When an act of discipline is used, the example needs to be one of loving kindness that meets the need of the person or situation.

Experience shows that much of this is easier said than done, because other factors enter the dynamic at this third stage, which alter things; in particular, the rise of the sex centre.

I have found it very important to do one's best to give parents the confidence that their sons and daughters will survive adolescence and puberty. Equally, it is important to help them navigate the staging posts through this 'Neanderthal experience'. The first piece of advice I always give is, 'Look to yourself. You survived, so there is hope for your offspring too!'

How to deal with the sexual development of youngsters is tricky and controversial. Shantaananda points out that the sex centre in the girl starts to rise at around twelve years old, but in boys it does not show itself until around fifteen or sixteen. In both genders an explosion of energy marks the time. Observation tends to confirm this perspective and I have often wondered whether the earlier growth of the sex centre in girls accounts for their inherent brightness and brilliance during adolescence. More recently, scientists have started to show that the growth and development of the brains of young boys and girls not only occurs differently, but it takes place at different speeds. Some psychologists are now suggesting that boys may not reach brain growth maturity until they are around twenty-five, whereas girls get there at eighteen. Were he alive today, Shantaananda would most probably nod in agreement.

The stage between ten and sixteen is also marked by a natural rise in desire for things and objects, not just sexually oriented, but usually powered by the same centre. As a consequence, an aspect of the mental realm begins to be exercised more. This is the 'monkey' aspect of mind – the part that constantly chases after things. Shantaananda compares this lower part of the mind to the more useful higher part, which he describes as pure intellect. The intellect is the realm of reason. It is the part of the mental apparatus that decides what is right and wrong, true and false, and so on. It has to be nourished with good material. He also points out that the sensory world covers this pure intellect with a world of its own, composed of 'what I want and don't want'. When the monkey mind, chasing after desires, is allowed to run free, never hearing the word no, it ultimately becomes frustrated.

The sense of invincibility quickly arises in a youthful chap, pepped up by his rise in testosterone, but suddenly for some reason he can't get what he wants, and now all that power turns to negativity and doubt. A few moments ago he was on the crest of a wave; now he is being dashed on the rocks. He feels in desperate need of another boost, and he will get this through his sensory channels, which work to serve the monkey mind. This is why he loves to plug into music, watch television, or play on his computer endlessly. Oh, how the word no becomes so important.

If from the age of ten to sixteen a youngster does not learn how to get some control over the monkey mind, he will never be able to develop his true intellectual capacity fully. Thus, exercises like falling still and connecting consciously with the sensory world are very important. Learning how to stop and empty the mind of all that stuff is equally important. When there is a conscious awareness (see chapter 2) as to what is happening to the mind, the intellect naturally fires up. The greatest food for the intellect is the power of awareness.

Schools are not meant to tackle all of this on their own. Parental involvement is essential. At the same time, parents ask us what they can do to help control this explosion of the sensory appetite. Advice has to be measured and a step-by-step approach should always be encouraged. Simple things can be suggested: not allowing youngsters to be continually plugged in to iPods and similar devices; not allowing them unfettered access to computers in their bedrooms, but ensuring that the devices are in a more common home space, like the kitchen; making sure that children have access to nature so they can use their senses in the way their Creator intended them to; taking them to enjoy the sensory delights of the best of theatre or great architectural feats in different towns and cities. All these things cultivate the proper use of the sensory mechanism, consciously and intelligently, and the result is to help keep the intellect, the seat of love and reason, clear of confusion. The rampant world of desire is brought under some measure of control.

Shantaananda says that at age sixteen, the fourth stage begins, when children transform into adults and, as a result, they need to be treated rather differently to when they were under sixteen. They need to be regarded as friends first and then offspring. To reach this new relationship, a preparatory phase is necessary, generally between age fourteen and sixteen. Don't expect the friendship thing to arise by itself; that has to be prepared for by giving the youngster some freedoms and responsibilities before he or she turns sixteen.

In my experience with boys, the actual birthday of the sixteen-year-old has been fascinating to watch. A week or so before the day, he is a gangly, testosterone-filled, fifteen-year-old vacuum of undirected energy. He doesn't seem to know who he is or what is happening to him. On the morning of his sixteenth birthday, he awakens as a different chap. He still knows nothing about being an adult, but he has clearly stepped into another world. The world of childhood has been left behind.

Some parents wonder whether this stage marks the end of their 'saying no' phase. My advice to them has been 'not quite.' It's best to treat your new friend as still inexperienced and still needing help and direction, but now, supporting your guidance with even more good reasons as to why not. It is still unreasonable to go out and party all night before school the next day. It is still unreasonable not to inform someone of where you are and who you are with – even mature adults do that.

At St James we mark the age of sixteen by allowing the boys to wear business suits and come out of school uniform. If their behaviour and work rates are reasonable, their teachers give them greater freedoms during the school day and more latitude with work. By the time they are eighteen and about to leave for university, they have the mental and emotional maturity of young men ready to face the world, full of confidence, courage, a sense of control, and some sense of their duty to society. If they are treated rather differently at home, it causes confusion and division; so if you, as head, follow this approach at school, it is very important to bring the parents on board. Our experience is that they are mightily grateful for your doing so.

Shortly before one of my parenting lectures, I presented a class of fourteen-year-old boys with an essay topic. I asked them to write about what they wanted from their parents. It is an interesting exercise, which I recommend.

The parental profile of our school is similar to that of the vast majority of independent schools in the UK. We have a clutch of wealthy parents, but the vast majority work every God-given hour to be able to afford our fees. Many, especially the Indian and Pakistani families, have local retail businesses in which the children participate, especially at the weekends. They do not come from the soft underbelly of the newly rich, but rather from families where education is of paramount importance to success in the world and societal progress.

The boys, almost without exception, began by expressing their gratitude to their parents for all they had been given, including their schooling. But equally, the vast majority of boys said that the one thing they wanted from their parents was time: time to do things together, time to go out together to the cinema or theatre, or time for a picnic together. The essays expressed the desire for a fair bit of testosterone-based independence too, but they loved spending time with their parents, especially when they'd had so little time together for so long.

One boy, who lived with his mother and step-father, wrote of how he loved seeing his natural father every other weekend. However, the father often had to work on Saturday mornings and Sunday afternoons, and he would give his son large sums of money to make up for this, money which ultimately got the boy into trouble when he spent it in one of London's notorious marketplaces. One of the greatest dangers in parenting is to think that money is a substitute for time and attention.

Another mistake so easily made by loving and caring parents is to take at face value everything their child says to them, as if it had the truth of gospel about it. I got wind that a fifteen-year-old was going to host a Saturday night party. His parents wanted to give him 'plenty of space' and decided to take themselves off for a romantic weekend at the coast, leaving the boy's twenty-one-year-old brother in charge. When I heard this, along with the fact that Facebook had a chain-invitation running, I picked up the phone to call the mother.

'Oh, he told me that only about twenty people will be there, and there would be no alcohol. After all, he is too young, isn't he?' she told me. I said nothing, and after a brief silence she said, 'You don't believe him, do you?'

'No', I replied, quickly adding that he might be intending it to be like that, but with parental absence, a substitute carer who certainly would want to have alcohol available for himself and his own friends (who she later admitted were also coming), the chances of this being an innocent affair were rather limited. She took the hint, cancelled her weekend away, and brought in three other sets of parents to help keep the affair civilised. On Monday she phoned me, full of gratitude. The place had been overrun with youngsters, many not invited, who had picked up from social media sites the fact that a 'rave' was about to happen at a parent-less location. After the daughter of one of the other parents present was man-handled by a group of older youths, the parents decided to call the police and disburse the affair. It ended relatively harmlessly, but the possibility of disaster was clear for them all to see.

'How did you know this was likely to happen?' she asked. I told her that having had three sons of my own had helped to sensitise the trouble-seeking antennae. Young people do not have the experience to be able to prevent some difficulties occurring, even if their intentions are good. Good parenting inevitably means being present at important times.

When parents question how their presence can be made more substantial without becoming intrusive in the life of an adolescent, I often ask them how many meals each week they have together as a family. I have to admit to being shocked at the response I frequently get. An extraordinary number of families no longer eat around the same table together, at any of the three meals of the day, even at weekends. Yet this is a simple and natural place for harmony and good conversation. It is also a good place for parents to detect if there are any hidden problems; even a grunting, grumpy, pimple-ridden youth cannot cover up a deep-seated problem, meal after meal. The parents are going to have to respond, even if it just means asking the school for help.

One father told one of our evening parenting groups how he consciously decided what topics to raise over dinner when everyone was together as a family. He was interested in current affairs and politics and would often preface a conversation on a topic with the question: 'So, what would you do if you were prime minister?' He had to try not to act like the chairman of the board and also had to be sure that he did not 'win' the argument. It was a dialogue, and everyone had a perfect right to his or her opinions. He would often stimulate the same kind of conversation when the family had guests to dinner. The result was that his sons had a rather universal outlook and were used to entering into conversation with adults. It also made mealtime very interesting and something to be looked forward to.

All good schools deliver programmes on sex, drugs, alcohol, and the use of the Internet. However, without ensuring that the same messages are delivered to the parents, the educational role is only half done.

We have a zero-tolerance policy at St James on drug use, either in or out of school, and the result is that the problem is minimised; but like all schools we have incidents to deal with. When a thirteen-year-old was excluded after failing a drugs test (an important weapon in the armoury of head teachers), his parents were totally shocked because they had seen no signs of his problem. Yet they did not know where he was until quite late at night, especially at the weekends, and even when they thought they knew (because he'd told them), he turned out to be somewhere else, doing something else with someone else. The police later told us that the place where the boy got his drugs had been a notorious trafficking spot for years and that all parents should be warned not to allow their sons to go there. We did this, via email, letter, and text, prior to calling a meeting. Only about a third of the parents from the affected age group turned up.

Boys openly tell us that they cannot go to night spots in and around London without being offered drugs. Colleagues from other metropolitan areas confirm the same experience. The drugs culture is everywhere. It is therefore vital that both parents and the school remain utterly vigilant and work together. Just as dangerous is the proliferation of alcohol amongst young people. It is not unusual for the drinking habit to begin as young as fourteen, and by the time the pressure of public exams comes around, from sixteen to eighteen, youngsters are consuming units of alcohol far above the level that is safe for their health. Of course, they don't pay much heed to statistics, nor do they think illness can happen to them. The message as to the dangers of frequent and excessive use of alcohol is an important one for the whole school community to grasp.

There is a curious thing about human beings. We don't seem to need to be educated in the things that are bad for us; we gravitate naturally towards them. So, as Shantaananda Saraswati said, it is important to get the good in early. The earliest influence is the parents.

Most of today's parents are themselves the product of a generation of parents who questioned nearly everything, at a time when technology was advancing extremely quickly but when it was still too early to know the impact on individuals and society of all the gadgetry now widely and cheaply available. My first car phone cost nearly £1500, and was an 'event'. Today, mobile phones with more computing power than was formerly available to NASA in sending men to the moon are now virtually disposable fashion items. What is the impact on our brains of endless mobile phone use? I would lay a bet that within twenty years the cancerous effects of excessive phone use will begin to be detected. Youngsters are perpetually plugged in to iPods and other sensory gadgets that blast stuff into their minds and brains for hours on end. Ride on a train, a plane, or a boat and the frequent sight is a youngster, myopically enthralled by flashing colour and lights, listening to harsh sounds for hours on end. It is rare to see a mother or father reading to a toddler or playing observation games to while away the hours. I would lay another bet that in a few years we will link this level of sensory bombardment with chronic attention deficit across vast oceans of society, which will in turn lead to the production of attention-enhancing drugs for the masses, not just for the children with Attention Deficit Disorder.

At St James Senior Boys' we have a rule: No iPods or listening devices on the journey to and from school. It is not a very good rule because it is so difficult to enforce, but I feel we have to do something to maintain the concentration. We notice that the boys' attention takes several hours to focus when they come to school on Monday mornings. We investigated and found that over the weekend they spend hours lying on their beds, listening to the gadgets or playing computer games.

What you put into the mind must have its effect. If you were to eat a bowl of poison, you would not expect it to pass through the body without trouble. Why is it, then, that we think our youngsters can continually plug in to an ever-increasingly agitated sensory experience without it affecting their power of attention?

I have never met a parent who wants less than the best for his or her offspring. I have, however, met many parents who do not know what to do to help educate them. They are aware that something going on around them needs to change and are keen to receive help and advice. I hold the view that it is part of our role as school leaders to provide it.

This is not a nicety to perform. It is essential if we are to form the quality of character that we want our pupils to embody by the time they leave our care and head into the world. If we take on this role, society one day will thank us, and the esteem in which teachers are held will have returned to its rightful premier position.

## Reflections on Care of the Parents

The SMT is encouraged to hold an away day dialogue on the role of parents in the school. Following are some of the questions that could be addressed:

- How consistent are the values of the parental body with the school's fundamental approach to building character?

- What more can be done for and with the parental body to sensitise them to the issues affecting the growth and development of their children?

- Is our Personal, Social and Health Education (PSHE) programme robust enough? How can the content of it more effectively enter into family life?

### Potential Essays/Discussions for Adolescents

Raising the issue of parenting is a potential new dimension in the PSHE programme. Essays could be set for pupils or discussions held on the following themes:

- When I become a parent, what will I do differently from what my own parents do in bringing up of a family? What will I emulate?

- Why is family important in society? What is the impact on society of the decline in the traditional concept of family?

- What should mothers and fathers do to make sure their children are happy? What are the main hurdles in making this happen?

## CHAPTER 11

# KEEPING FIT

FORTUNATELY, I HAVE ALWAYS LOVED the early mornings. Equally fortunately, my life has found itself so organised that either inner or outer compulsion has conspired to get me out of bed on most days around the crack of dawn.

As a youngster I lived in a New Zealand town close to the surfing hot spots. With a good heave on the pedals I could cycle from home to Fitzroy Beach by around 5.30 a.m. and catch the glassiest of waves for a couple of hours before school. I have to confess to staying on the water beyond the call of the school bells on numerous occasions, but I must also confess that on nearly every one of those occasions I managed to persuade the school's registration secretary that I had been engaged on important school business; hence my attendance record remained exemplary. The charming woman probably went to her grave in total admiration at my deep interest in collecting seaweed samples for biology, or sand samples for my study on the impact of wind on erosion for geography!

Later, after qualifying as a journalist and turning to broadcasting, I found myself on the early morning news shift, which again gave plenty of time to either return to the waves or play squash with my technician, a wonderful woman who had the additional virtue of considerable attractiveness.

I was delighted, therefore, when my philosophical mentor introduced me at around age twenty-one to the practise of meditation, and advised that the best times of the day to come to deep inner rest were dawn and as the sun was starting to set.

'These are the most *sattvic* (swan-like energy) times', he would tell us. 'Dawn and dusk are the best times to meditate and gain peace. It's easy. Just get up when you wake up. Shower and find a comfortable seat. Close the eyes and start to meditate. Sit in the same way at the end of the day. Half an hour of this and you will feel rejuvenated'.

A number of my friends found it hard enough to wake up when they got up, let alone do it the other way round. But I was lucky. I'd had years of practice of early mornings and so eagerly took to the new discipline.

By this time I had moved to the United Kingdom, not world renowned for surfing opportunities, so the temptation of surfing and meditating simultaneously (something I now believe is entirely possible!) was not available. Instead, I would shower as quickly as possible, find a nice comfortable seat, close my eyes, and begin.

At the start, my flat-mates thought I was completely mad. Meditation was just catching on, thanks to Maharishi Mahesh Yogi and the Beatles. Some elders in the Church thought it was the work of the devil. Some people thought it was a precursor to or a cover-up for a 'trip' of another kind. Still, if you just follow the crowd you will never find the space you need as an individual, so I happily kept practising.

I found at the beginning a depth of inner peace never before experienced, even through prayer. It was very akin to that feeling of utter contentment and bliss that occasionally occurs after a night of deep sleep, often following a day of very hard physical work. I thought, 'I could stay here forever'.

After a couple of months, however, something seemed to change. I started to notice that my mind was like a vacuum that filled on a regular basis with waves of thoughts. There were thoughts about what was to come later that day; thoughts about what had happened the day or month before, and my part in it all. Then there were thoughts about 'me': whether I was any good at anything; whether I could maintain a relationship. And questions: Would life descend into one round of drunken nights after another? Could something better happen? The thoughts were always random but always had the same effect. If they were believed, as they usually were when they were appearing, they sucked and sapped an enormous amount of energy.

My meditation guide at the time was a gentle, other-worldly soul who made his living as a professional artist. I would visit his home, often early on Sunday mornings, and we would enjoy the most delicious coffee and buns and chat about life and the role of meditation in it. He would always laugh when I pointed out how I had failed miserably day after day with my meditation; how I had started with such clarity and inner peace, but now would finish a session wracked with guilt and exhausted from so many ideas. The more I spoke, the more hilarious he seemed to find it.

Finally, one day, he looked up and said, 'Actually, you are meditating very well, because you are seeing what is happening in your mind. Most people can't or won't do that. All you need to do now is to stop believing in these ideas that appear while you are meditating. Remember, you are not these ideas. You are not even your mind. You are the Witness of them. Just learn to watch and let them go. You will find that the peace you met when you began will return.'

I decided to try it. Initiating a new level of patience with myself, I started to watch the movements of my mind and not believe them. 'Believing' in thoughts is always evidenced by being affected by them, usually negatively. I discovered that I could just watch the thoughts, let them go on their own, and return the attention to the mantra, or special sound, I had been given when I was introduced to meditation.

The word mantra is interesting. It is a Sanskrit word composed of two elements: *man* (which rhymes with sun) means 'mind' (and is also the source of the word 'man'), and *tra* means 'release'. So a mantra is that which gives you release from your mind.

Now if there is something most headmasters feel they need, it is release from the burdens of their job, which are mainly burdens lodged in the mind. I discovered this when, quite late at night at a Society of Heads conference, I delicately tried to sneak away from the bar to go to bed, because I wanted to get up early in the morning to meditate before making a presentation. (It is always good to prepare mentally and emotionally for such events.) The flurry of banter as I left the drinking school prompted me to give the real reason for my early departure, and just as I was feeling a bit pompous and ridiculous, a couple of the heads asked, 'Can you teach us to meditate?' Another colleague interrupted and said she wanted to join too.

'Okay', I said, fairly convinced they were not at all serious. 'Here's my room number. I'll start at 6.00 a.m. and you would be very welcome to join me'. I did not expect them to turn up, but sure enough, at the appointed hour there was a knock on the door and there they were – fit, keen, and eager to be released from the burdens of the mind.

Around an hour and a half later, refreshed and enthused, they said, 'You know, this is a tremendous way to start the day. You should write a book about all of this stuff because we need to know about it!'

The mantra technique of meditation is just one of many, but it is very effective. The special sound, which is given by a master or guru, occupies the attention, allowing you to leave everything else. The sound of your mantra leads you back to a place of deep stillness and inner rest, an oasis in the midst of a turbulent world. The technique involves sounding the mantra inwardly with full attention, but without excessive effort. When it is moving along, repeating evenly, and you have given it momentum, you just let it go into the space of the mind. 'Let go ... let go ... let go', is the refrain of all good meditation teachers. Now listen ... listen all the way through the sound and be aware of where the sound is going. You are the power of witnessing, the power of awareness.

You may have seen a young boy, crouched at the side of a small lake with his model sailing boat beautifully rigged and ready to sail.

He is aware of the direction of the breeze, and all that is needed to let his boat sail away is a gentle push. So too with this form of meditation. The mantra is the model sailing boat. Your attention is the power of momentum. So, with full attention, gently push the mantra out into the ocean of the mind, listen, and remain aware of what is happening.

This technique, when practised regularly, begins to reveal how we live our lives. We perpetually hold on to things in our minds, and letting them go is not so easy. We love to get involved with events, people, and experiences, and that involvement first happens in the mind.

The ancient sages did not intend humankind to use the mind to tie itself in knots. Their vision was that the mind is a much freer and more spacious condition, an experience or 'atmosphere' of lightness and illumination, not one filled with multiple and conflicting things. Their vision was for the mind to be a brilliant reflector of the divine power of consciousness and awareness, not an independent mechanical instrument that ignores its source.

The odd thing is that none of us has ever grasped the mind as an independent entity. We have noticed plenty of ideas, but no one has ever located his mind in his body. We think it is in the head, because that is where the brain is. But when an autopsy is conducted, whether on a Nobel prize-winner or a street cleaner, our brains are found to be pretty much the same size and constituted of the same billions of neurones and hormonal channels. So the mind is of a different, more subtle order than the brain, and yet the two aspects work entirely together.

The scientific community is beginning to find out much more about the impact of meditation on the levels of human happiness, the release of stress, and the changes that occur to the physiological and neurological systems when the mind concentrates for a prolonged period – on a mantra, for example.

Dr Shanida Nataraj, whose PhD is in Neurophysiology from University College, London, and who is a regular meditator and yoga practitioner, explains in her book, *The Blissful Brain*, that the main physical link between our bodies and our minds is the network of nerve cells that produce and secrete hormones into the bloodstream, known as the neuro-endocrine system. The release of different hormones is triggered by activity in the brain, and therefore, changes in brain activity can drive changes in the body's functioning. In her view, stress, a condition suffered by many heads, can trigger long-term abnormalities in the neuro-endocrine system, including an abnormal increase in the level of cortisol, the stress hormone itself. The link between stress and mood is also thought to be the result of the amount of serotonin in the brain: the state of happiness is associated with increased levels of serotonin, and depression is associated with decreased levels of the hormone. Her work is beginning to show that meditation practised on a regular basis not only changes the structure of the brain, primarily by balancing its two hemispheres, but also significantly reduces stress levels and advances human health.

The left hemisphere of the brain contains the neuronal system associated with written and spoken language and is often thought to be the dominant hemisphere. It does the analytical, rational, and logical processing, something most of us seem to use most of the time and which we as teachers are usually keen to develop. The right hemisphere, however, contains the regions associated with abstract thought and emotion. It is often under-developed and shows as deficient in what has come to be termed 'emotional intelligence'. Emotional intelligence is that intuitive instinct which allows human relationships to flourish naturally. Its power is enhanced by connection with stillness through meditation.

An article in the medical journal, *The Lancet*, in the early 1970s, highlighted research that measured the breathing rates of two control groups: one of people who were doing a form of transcendental meditation and another of people who were not meditating. The meditators recorded an average of six breaths per minute while the non-meditating group recorded around twelve. The breathing pattern of the meditators paralleled a drop in the metabolic rate of around 75%. Reducing the number of breaths per minute, with an increase in the depth of each breath, is an ideal held out by meditation teachers, particularly in the Eastern traditions. They teach that breath is connected to the mind, through the brain. If the breath slows down, the movement of the mind slows down too, and the level of stress experienced is reduced.

An article in *Science* (Volume 167: 1751-4) showed that meditators experience a decrease in their heart rate of about five beats per minute and a decrease in the amount of blood pumped by the heart of about 25%. Both phenomena indicate a state of deep inner rest; this stress-free state can carry over into everyday life. Over 200 studies conducted over the past thirty years show that people who meditate regularly are generally more relaxed, fitter, and freer of much of the stress of life as a result of their meditation.

Alongside that is testimony from many meditators, quoted throughout Dr Nataraj's book, and certainly confirmed by my own experience, that one effect of meditation is to lose the sense of 'not having enough time' and 'being separate from everything else.' Timelessness and spaciousness are conducive to meditative peace and certainly very helpful in simply letting everything go.

As heads we need to find some way, every day, to release the pressures of the job and to keep our bodies and minds in a fit and healthy condition. Finding the right amount of time is always the challenge, but there is a key for this too.

'I don't have time' turns out to be an enormously powerful *idea*, which, if dropped, actually releases time. At first, it appears like an irresolvable riddle: 'I need more time, but to get more time, I have to give time to letting all ideas go.' To find out how this works, an element of faith is needed at the beginning.

My personal experience has shown that giving twenty to thirty minutes a day to meditative practice, say half in the morning and half in the evening, creates more mental and emotional space to attend to all the things that are required. A minute is a very long time when it is consciously considered. Just sit and watch the second hand of a clock for a full minute, without attending to anything else, and you will discover this.

Every head needs to create time. One of Rudyard Kipling's famous phrases puts it well: 'Sixty seconds worth of distance run'. Creating time does not mean to stop doing certain things, because we know from experience and observation that that tends not to happen. It really means making each minute last a minute – to be there, present, in the moment.

As the day gets underway, we often observe that the pace seems to increase. More and more is asked of us, often with multiple requests occurring at the same time, resulting in more opportunities for pressure and tension. If we can stop the build-up of pressure as we go, by finding a way to keep releasing tensions continuously, the run-down takes longer and the recovery happens more quickly. At St James, we work with what we call *The Pause* (see chapter 3). Before any activity begins, we take a minute to stop, reconnect with our sensory apparatus, and bring our minds into the present moment. We do this at the beginning and end of every lesson and at the beginning and end of lunch. When we meet as a leadership team, we do it at the beginning and end of every meeting. The mind is encouraged to drop everything that is happening in it and to focus back to the present moment.

One simple way of 'pausing' is just to stop whatever you are doing, take a seat somewhere, and consciously reconnect with your breath and the sights and sounds around you. To do that, you have to stop thinking about what you were thinking about a minute ago. You can't think about what is to come, because if you do you will not reconnect with your present; you will just stay 'thinking' about things or possibilities in the past or future. *The Pause* is the release valve on the mental pressure cooker, and the beauty is that it can take place at any time and in any circumstance. It certainly helps to close the eyes for part or all of the time, but it is not essential. What is important is the connection in the present moment to the present moment.

When I first started to use this practice of pausing in the early 1970s, I felt extremely self-conscious about it. I would take myself to the toilets at work and make a 'thing' of it. Then I saw Arthur

Ashe, the first world-renowned African-American tennis player, play in the 1975 Wimbledon final. At the changeover he would go to his seat, close his eyes, and focus. He was thirty-one at the time, and clearly moving towards the end of his career, yet each time he came back onto the court refreshed, centred, and in control. He was not just beating his opponent with great racket work. He seemed to be pausing, dropping, what had just happened, and staying absolutely attentive to the present. From that day on I thought, 'If Arthur Ashe can pause in front of the Centre Court crowd and millions of tennis fans on TV, I can pause at my desk too!' What I have observed is that most people are far too absorbed in their own worlds to notice what you are doing.

My meditation mentor said one way to break the habit of thinking you never have enough time to attend upon mindfulness practices is to use things you regularly engage in to trigger the memory to do it. My job at the time involved taking frequent taxi rides. Every time I opened the door of the taxi to get into it, I remembered to STOP AND PAUSE – SAP! I used to enjoy the pause so much that it would frequently drift into a short period of meditation, which is a brilliant way to take a taxi journey around London and so much more restful than worrying about the meeting you are going to. I have mentioned this technique to others and they have tried various things: remember SAP when you are brushing your teeth; remember SAP when you are picking up the telephone receiver or mobile; remember SAP when you turn over the correspondence file in the morning. Also, remember SAP as soon as you wake up in the morning, before the thoughts begin.

(Incidentally, one way to stop stress arising is to discipline yourself never to have to re-read correspondence. Read it – deal with it! It saves hours of both physical time and anxiety.)

One of the challenges in headship is that everyone expects you to be on the top of your game all of the time. You can't afford to have a bad meeting with a parent or not be on top form when that difficult discussion with the departmental head takes place. Fortunately, children are far more forgiving. When the assembly is terrible, they know there will be another one soon enough, and when it comes, they blessedly don't hold the last poor performance against you. It is important, therefore, for the head to keep fit in all the worlds: physical, mental, and emotional.

Many heads spend far too much time in a sedentary position. Even if they regularly walk around the school, the majority of their day will be spent sitting and meeting someone or attending paperwork behind a desk. Regular physical exercise is a must, but it need not be too stressful on the physical body. Medical experts say that regular periods of walking, quite briskly and with some effort, can achieve tremendous aerobic, body-tuning, healthful results.

Two other exercises to be recommended are yoga and Pilates. There are many expert teachers available for both disciplines and they both have tremendous physical value. In addition, they involve concentration and focus, so they have a mental and emotional value too. I would underline from experience how important it is to find a teacher for either of these disciplines to avoid the risk of bodily injury and derive the maximum benefit.

For the last twenty years, the cult of running or jogging and working out at the gym has progressively gained ground, but taken alone it is a one-dimensional response to the need to keep fit. The ancient Vedas, the Eastern scriptures thousands of years old, dealt with the same issue. Much of this knowledge has found itself translated through Ayurveda (the Science of Health), an alternative system of health based on the balance of diet and energy. Guidance to individuals needs to be specific, but the general principles are worth noting.

Diet and our ability to digest the food we eat are of real importance in maintaining physical and mental health. Our ability to digest is affected by many things, including the time we eat and the kind of foods we consume. Meat products take far longer to digest (sometimes up to three days) as distinct from vegetable foods (as little as three hours). We have an inner digestive fire and if we keep putting it out by consuming too many cold liquids at the time of eating, the digestion will slow down. When digestion slows, the body accumulates what is called *ama*. A sign of this is that horrid sticky substance we scrape off our tongues in the morning, before we brush our teeth. The digestive energies are most powerful at around mid-day, so the best time to have the largest meal is around lunchtime.

Another principle of staying healthy, and to aid digestion, is to ensure that you leave space in the stomach for the digestion to take place, about a third. One guideline is to eat until you know you could eat more but shouldn't; another guideline is the amount of food that would fill both hands cupped together is your measure. Most of us can be certain it is far less than we normally eat.

Sleep and sleeping patterns are crucial to personal health and fitness. Not only will worry and stress cause you to lose energy and health over a mid-term, but going to bed too late or not getting up early enough plays its part too. The best sleep occurs during the two hours before and after midnight, when the same energy that digests food during the waking day is used to prepare for elimination from the body and release any mental and emotional toxins. That is why Ayurvedic health experts emphasise that the call to the 'loo' in the early morning is so important and if the bodily elimination is not full and complete, health problems inevitably arise. Sleeping too long causes the mind to enter a dream world, which saps energy. So the principle is to get up when you wake up.

When I was a younger man, my sleeping pattern was a clockwork affair. After four hours and twenty-three minutes, night after night, I would awaken, exceptionally bright and raring to go. Such an ability was of great assistance when working for Mrs T. After four hours of sleep, she would get up and start work, so when we were on the road together, after meditation, I would join her for some one-on-one time over the morning papers. It was a great time of day to look at things together, with nobody else around.

As the years passed, the sleep requirement lengthened, but not by much. Getting up around 5.30 a.m. gives me time for meditation and Pilates, before eating a quick, light breakfast and heading off for school. If the routine is disturbed, or if for some unusual reason the meditation cannot take place, I feel it.

During the course of the working day, the head transmits limitless amounts of energy, some of it physical, but much of it subtle and emotional. If he does not find some way to restore his energy, not just during the holidays, but also on a daily basis, he is going to collapse at some point.

The gods of health have so far been extremely kind to me. I have deliberately kept away from modern medicines and I have tried to live, as well as I can, according to the principles outlined in this book. When the common cold comes, usually in February, it does not last long. One winter, however, about four years into the job, the common cold was far worse than usual, and despite all the meditation, breathing techniques, and exercise, I could not shake it. It got worse and worse until I was in serious danger of having to take some time off school. What the doctor found was not pretty and he called for an immediate change of lifestyle. I had stopped smoking several years earlier, but now he wanted an immediate reduction, and preferably elimination, of the regular consumption of alcohol.

'If you don't stop now you will kill yourself', were his gentle words, which went into me like a dagger.

Here I was, a meditator who would get up early and do various exercises, being told to stop drinking because it was killing me.

'But I don't drink that much', I plaintively told him.

'Stop, or you will pay the price', he replied.

I went away and decided to look, as dispassionately as I could, at the levels of my alcohol intake. I was horrified. If I was to be brutally honest with myself, I was becoming an old soak. What I saw was that a headmaster can find an excuse to drink alcohol every day of the week. 'Well, if I open a bottle of wine, it will help the meeting go more smoothly', the thinking would go. When I could not find an external excuse, the inner excuse was that no one was scheduled to see me so I could now relax and a bottle of wine would help me do it. So I largely stopped, save the occasional celebratory glass of champagne. The result is that I have felt far healthier; I have also stopped falling asleep after dinner, thereby saving at least another hour in the day.

I have found it necessary to take some more straightforward physical exercise, which I would encourage so long as you choose something that does not allow excessive thinking at the same time. A clutch of heads are regular joggers, but many more swim or go cycling. And then of course, there is golf!

Common sense says that every school head should be encouraged to have an annual medical check-up. Keeping fit is a holistic issue, involving the body, mind, heart, and spirit. Nobody is going to tell the head what to do, so it will be a matter of inner discipline. As Oscar Wilde once said, 'In the long run, we are all dead'. But on the way, the head has a duty to himself and those in his care to look after himself, in all the worlds.

## Help to Keep Fit

### Meditation Exercises

Chapter 2 outlines a number of these exercises. Below are a few more.

#### Contemplative Prayer: 'I am Pure, Perfect, Free, Forever'

1. Find a comfortable seat and close your eyes.
2. Focus the attention on the space between your eyebrows or envision a space in the centre of your heart. Spend a minute just *being aware* of that space.
3. Engage with listening and listen all the way through the inner space to the silence that surrounds it. Give yourself time.
4. When you are in the silence, allow the words to appear in your conscious mind: 'I am Pure, Perfect, Free, Forever'. Repeat those words gently. Listen all the way through and allow some space at the end of one repetition before the next one begins.

If you practice this form of contemplative prayer regularly, you will notice that the time spent just staying with the inner space will expand and the number of repetitions of the phrase will reduce. This is evidence of your progress towards the Silence that permeates all space, where the deepest rest can be found.

Some who have practised this form of meditation regularly also speak of how it challenges other ideas of 'me' held by the ego. It is a particularly powerful form of meditation for a head who is not certain of himself, or who feels under pressure to improve his performance. It challenges the limited mind by ensuring that it dwells on a larger, more true idea.

## Christian Meditation

This form of meditation is particularly effective for those who connect with the Christian tradition. It is taught by the World Community for Christian Meditation. The Community recommends the following technique:

1. Sit down. Sit still and upright.
2. Close your eyes, lightly. Sit relaxed, but alert, with the back as straight as possible. Make sure there is no tension. If there is, just spend a moment to let it go.
3. Silently, within yourself, say a single word. The Community recommends the prayer-phrase *Maranatha*. Recite it as four syllables of equal length: *Ma-Ra-Na-Tha*.
4. Listen as you repeat it gently, but continuously. Try not to think or imagine anything, spiritual or otherwise. If thoughts or distractions come, gently return to the mantra, *Maranatha*.

The Community recommends meditating each morning and evening for between twenty and thirty minutes.

## The Pause

Either sitting or standing, just stop! Close the eyes or keep them open, whatever you are comfortable with. Then immediately start to connect with your sensory apparatus:

1. Feel the weight of your body seated on the chair or standing on the floor. *Feel it.*
2. Sense the play of air across your face and hands. *Feel it.*
3. Open to the world of scents and smells. *Smell it.*
4. Notice the world of tastes in your mouth. *Taste it.*
5. Let the listening be aware of everything. Listen to the sounds in the room. Listen to the sounds outside of the room. Listen to the sounds in the outside world. Now,

try to listen beyond all the physical sounds to the sound of silence. *Listen, listen, listen.*

6. Finally, allow all colours and forms of light to enter the vision. Just receive colour and light. Do nothing with it. *Receive the light ... just receive.*

In this exercise, allow space between each step and try not to be rushed. If you don't have much time, even thirty seconds of this, focussing on one or two of the senses, can be very helpful to become centred and focussed.

## Breathing Through to Relax

This is a breathing exercise specifically designed to re-lease tensions and bring forth the spirit of relaxation.

Either sitting or standing still, with eyes open or closed, inwardly follow the directions given below, giving time to each of them. (Try to learn them by heart.)

Say the phrases below quietly, inwardly, and attentively to yourself, and then follow them:

*Breathing in a short breath, I know I am breathing in ...*
(Follow the breath.)

*Breathing out a short breath, I know I am breathing out ...*
(Follow the breath.)

*Breathing in a long breath, I know I am breathing in ...*
(Follow the breath.)

*Breathing out a long breath, I know I am breathing out ...*
(Follow the breath.)

*Breathing in, I am aware of my whole body ...*
(Follow this awareness.)

*Breathing out, I am aware of my whole body ...*
(Follow this awareness.)

*Breathing in, I release tensions from my head and neck ...*
(Follow this release.)

*Breathing out, I release tensions from my head and neck ...*
(Follow this release.)

*Breathing in, I release tensions from my arms and torso ...*
(Follow this release.)

*Breathing out, I release tensions from my arms and torso ...*
(Follow this release.)

*Breathing in, I release tensions from my hips and legs ...*
(Follow this release.)

*Breathing out, I release tensions from my hips and legs ...*
(Follow this release.)

*Breathing in, I release tensions from my ankles and feet ...*
(Follow this release.)

*Breathing out, I release tensions from my ankles and feet ...*
(Follow this release.)

*Breathing in a deep breath, I bring the whole of my body
back into view ...*
(Follow this vision.)

*Breathing out, I release all the tensions ... release ... release.*

Repeat this as many times as you like. If you become aware of specific tensions in certain parts of the body, direct the attention there and stay focussed until the tension is released.

You can also use a short form of the exercise at any time. Ensure you practice both short and long breathing, however, and stay aware.

CHAPTER 12

# THE EARTH WON'T STOP TURNING

THROUGHOUT MY CAREER I SEEM to have specialised in committing faux pas.

The first was as a trainee journalist on a local New Zealand paper, read by half a town of farmers and a few of their sheep and cows. The local council had a great story about how the district tax rates were going to skyrocket – so I thought. Even the news editor's serious questioning of my interpretation of the figures caused me no hesitation. Confidence was at a peak and my first front page scoop was on its way.

Unfortunately, only *after* publication did I decide to closely read the small print guidance provided by the town clerk, finding to my total horror that far from the taxes increasing and causing a scandal, they were decreasing! The mayor, a big, beefy, pitchforking pig-farmer, who clearly had not heard of the Buddha's enlightenment, nor his teachings on harmlessness to all creatures, was out to get the cub reporter who had upset his great day of political glory. But even he was not as fierce as my editor, whose withering comments about my inabilities as a mathematician and political analyst are not fit for a mixed readership.

I took a full blast of Mrs T's caustic comments when, after a radio phone-in programme, my notes on 'prospective' callers were left in the studio, only to be found by the programme presenter. As the horror began to dawn that his 'spontaneous' phone-in had in fact been quite successfully managed by the spin doctor, praise from the Conservative news machine's hierarchy quickly turned to opprobrium. From saint to sinner in one short moment, as another news story seemed to be on the cards: 'Tory Spin Doctor Dupes Radio Station.'

This head's life has had its fair share of disastrous moments. For example, introducing a visiting head-teacher from a feeder school by the wrong name, and later linking his headship to the wrong school; or interviewing a pupil who I thought was somebody else and compounding the problem by phoning his rather perplexed parents with a load of information that made no sense to them at all. (At least in the latter situation, both boys had the same, rather common, surname!)

Life, if lived fully and adventurously, will be peppered with mistakes which, at the time, look and feel tremendously difficult and disastrous. But the fact is they are not. Several pages could be filled with similar disasters, but they have all passed, and probably the only person who really remembers them is me.

This is a very important principle in leadership. Nothing in the material world – the world of things and people and shapes and forms – is permanent. Spiritual teachers call this the law of impermanence, and it is a wonderful law to try to understand more fully because it sets you free to try to do things that you might otherwise not attempt.

Impermanence is all around us. Harsh though it may sound, from the moment a child is born he is heading towards the grave. It is an inevitability. Parents never keep their children, because time ensures that they grow and leave home and make their own lives. The time our children are with us as children is impermanent.

Our jobs are impermanent, and certainly our plans and successes are. I visited a prominent boys' public school, and the head proudly showed me the Honours Board listing all the previous heads. Most had spent ten or twelve years in the job over the past 150 years; a couple had important school buildings named after them, but the majority were neither remembered nor particularly cared for. When they were in post, they must have been significant men because the heritage left by them, as evidenced by the school today, is extremely impressive. But their specific achievements had passed from remembrance, because they, and their successes and mistakes, were impermanent.

It is too often the fear of making mistakes, and the associated concern that they will somehow damage us and our reputations, that cause so many heads to wait for too long before doing with their schools what they want to do or what they know needs to be done. The result of this condition is that the independent educational sector in the UK is becoming too bland and 'me-too-ish'. If this trend continues – and it is in danger of doing so – we will lose our revered worldwide status as world-class educational providers.

I am not advancing a reckless approach to educational development, but I am encouraging the next generation of school heads to make best use of their independence whilst they have it, whether they are in the private or state sectors.

That independence is being threatened, stealthily, by the day. It is tempting to think that those governing us are not aware of it, but I fear the educational policymakers are very conscious of what is happening to the fee-paying independent sector. Over the last few years, since coalition politics overcame our age-old political stereotypes, the words used by politicians and bureaucrats to describe the national educational scene have sought to confuse the general public about what 'independent' education is. The fee-paying independent sector, fractured into several semi-competitive groupings as it is, has done very little to counter that confusion.

Free Schools, a generally positive development in the state sector, are openly described by government ministers as 'independent', despite the fact they do not have a freedom of admission policy. The academy sector, still directly under government control and still little different in form from the old 'comprehensives', is also now heralded for its new 'independence'.

I am all for 'independence', in whichever form it presents itself, but I suspect as the Free Schools and academy sector start to mature, the reality of their lack of independence will show, especially once the political climate changes. They will not be able to innovate in the way that the fee-paying sector will need to do if it is to continue to thrive and lead the way. Innovation will not come from policies; it will come from spirited and adventurous head teachers who are confident in themselves and in their abilities to meet the real needs of the children in front of them. They will also need to be confident in delivering a new educational approach designed to meet the needs and challenges of the twenty-first century, which are far greater than anything the technology revolution can address. Indeed, in education, the so-called technology revolution could be seen as a driver to many of its problems.

Greater use of computers and their associated technologies by both pupils and teachers has been the response to many educational issues over the last decade. Poor classroom teaching – clearly identified by Ofsted (Office for Standards in Education, Children's Services and Skills) in an inspectorate's report – has been tackled by creating an expectation that a child will learn best sitting in a classroom with an interactive white board, allowing the teacher to spend much of the lesson distracting his attention with videos or games. And yet it is the youngsters' ever-increasing use of iPods, computer games, and endless visual and auditory stimuli, such as what comes through their mobile phones, that is creating the most serious educational challenge of our modern age – a widespread inability to concentrate and keep the power of attention focussed. A national attention deficit is being experienced in classrooms up and down the country. Every teacher knows it, but there is a remarkable reluctance to admit it.

We are creating a generation of youngsters who simply cannot attend to anything in front of them, other than for the shortest of periods. I am not talking about those whose inability to attend and general agitation is so great that they are specifically classified as having Attention Deficit Hyperactivity Disorder (ADHD) or something similar. While they too are increasing in number and must be helped, here I am referring to the vast majority of children in our care.

I hold the view that continually plugging in to devices that cause the mind to be agitated is the real cause of this problem, and so at St James Senior Boys', we have adopted the policy of confiscating earphones from our pupils wherever we come across them and ban their use on the journeys to and from school (also noted in chapter 10). The long summer holidays, in this respect, are deadly.

The inability to attend has a series of spiritual, emotional, and mental consequences. At the spiritual level, when attention cannot be sustained, it is not possible to meet the depth of the person in front of you. Even worse, you can only live in the circling inner world of your own imaginations, isolated from reality, and self-indulgent, in your own dreams. Instead of the world being seen to be a glorious expression of divine beauty, with oceans of stillness and space in which to rest your Being, it becomes a rapidly passing show of colour and form, endlessly on the move and perpetually stressful.

The ancient sages advised that to achieve a measure of spiritual rest requires the ability to watch the movements of the mind and not be taken along with them. That is not possible without steady concentration. They also advised that mental rest would be achieved when the space between ideas and desires in the mind could be expanded. That too would require the power of concentration.

At the mental level, knowledge cannot be unfolded without the attention being in place, and that demands an inner focussing of the consciousness. Our response to our children's increasingly failing abilities to attend has been to put before them more of the very thing that is causing the problem – distractive colour and light and sounds in the form of 'visual aids' and 'gimmicks' in the classroom. It is like feeding a sick man with poison. We will not really know about its full effects until the current generation of hyper-cyber kids become parents and cannot attend to their own children or look after us properly in our old age. The prospective level of misery is considerable, and unless we really start to do something about it now, our society as we know it will be broken.

The emotional impact of inattentiveness has probably the most devastating effect on the character development of our youngsters. Their inability to attend to anything seriously, to penetrate beyond the surface, leads to their inner feeling of doubt and lack of self-belief. Never being able to be certain of whether something is true or not leads to an inevitability of living in a world of relativities. A world without certainties or absolutes of any kind is an ever-shifting realm. As the uncertainty increases, the slipping and sliding from one superficial experience to another, chasing inner satisfaction where it is not, magnifies the lack of faith in themselves still further. Inevitably, the satisfaction being craved is never found because lasting contentment can never be experienced through the shifting things. This lack of power to concentrate will lock our youngsters into a world of disappointment and frustration, leading in turn to inner anger and still more desire for things to dream about in the pursuit of happiness.

Chasing after happiness in the outer ephemeral world of material objects is a direct consequence of not being able to sustain attention and penetrate to the heart of any matter. As sensory objects are always moving and changing, the level of satisfaction to be found there is limited. This is one reason why the sages of old guided the original educationalists to prepare their charges to practice control of the senses and turn inward towards self-discovery through meditation. Self-discovery is not possible if the power to turn away from the outer sensory world does not exist.

When practices in strengthening the powers of attention and concentration are offered to youngsters, their spirits are immediately lifted.

I asked our learning support people to arrange some simple calligraphy lessons for our boys with ADHD. The teacher, who clearly understood the importance of simple attentiveness and knew how to encourage it, got the handful of boys to draw straight lines and circles on paper on an upright board held at a forty-five-degree angle. She ensured that they had the right nibs and that they were properly tutored in the art of holding the pen. This in turn called for an ability to be in the present moment; any inattention would cause the pen to be gripped like a vice and the ink would simply fail to flow. The simplicity of the technique was startling, but so was the effectiveness.

A short time later, the boys were beginning to be able to repeat a series of lines and circles, which soon led to the shapes of letters and some of the most beautiful written script you could imagine. The boys were delighted.

There was another unexpected spin-off. Because physical space was so tight, the exercise had to take place in a corridor leading to the main hall. This meant that vast numbers of the general pupil body had to walk past the lads at their calligraphy boards. Because the work was clearly so enjoyable and so beautiful, the passers-by inevitably stopped, looked more closely, and asked questions. The boys, calligraphy pens in hand, loved being able to show their work with pride. Their self-esteem rose, as did a touch of envy from the other boys, who, before long were asking for calligraphy lessons too.

We have now embraced the exercise in the Year 7 curriculum: every boy gets the chance to hold a free-flowing calligraphy pen and draw the most exquisite letters. We also maintain the school policy that the boys should not use laptops for producing their work until they reach the sixth form (with exceptions made for those who are physically challenged). Instead, they all have to use fountain pens and receive good, clear advice directing their attention to where the nib of the pen is meeting the paper. The knowledge will simply flow, they are told, if their attention is settled at that point, known as the point of interaction. To their great delight, they discover that by giving real attention to that point, the knowledge does flow, as if by itself. Moreover, they can apply their experience of focussing the attention to other areas and gain still more joy and knowledge.

There is a direct correlation between the pupil's ability to acquire or discover knowledge and the pupil's ability to attend and concentrate. We know that even the simplest of actions benefits greatly by having real attention paid to it. The task is not only more effective, but also the level of satisfaction from it significantly increases.

The next generation of headmasters and headmistresses needs to focus their pedagogy more on helping pupils to strengthen their powers of attention, rather than embracing methodologies and artificial aids, including drug therapy, to overcome the paucity of attentiveness. This next generation of 'independent' heads will have to take far greater risks and be far more courageous than we have had to be over the past fifty years, to ensure that their pupils actually receive the knowledge they need and develop their characters to be suitable for meeting the world's challenges. This is because the next generation of heads will have to face new challenges to education, posed by technology and science, even while embracing the benefits they offer.

Drug manufacturers have already tuned in to this national attention deficit. An increasing number of non-ADHD students at some of our leading universities have started to discuss the use of Ritolin and other similar chemical substances to enhance their performance during examinations. It is a scandal waiting to be exposed. Just as the world's sports authorities have clamped down on high-profile athletes using performance-enhancing substances, so too will the world's leading universities soon have to reveal the extent of this problem and how they will react to their student cohort who are drinking, injecting, or otherwise ingesting mind-enhancing drugs, especially on the eve of university exams.

Many challenges are presented by this phenomenon to everyone at the secondary school level. Whatever is accepted at the universities quickly filters into the behaviour patterns of those about to join them. Admissions tutors already face enormous challenges to identify and select the outstanding students from the many who are simply very good. What will happen to the system when A-level eighteen-year-olds, knowing the difficulty of getting a place at university, pop pills to get themselves better results with a minimum of extra effort? The increasingly discredited league tables will be even more meaningless, the parental body even more difficult to satisfy, and the pupils, who generally know who is 'on the game' and who is not, even more cynical and dispirited.

Along with the crisis of the national attention deficit has come a distorted view of the nature of knowledge and a diminishing level of importance as to the part it plays in the whole educational process.

The arrival of 'Mr Google' type features on every conceivable electronic gadget has led to an increasing view in the classroom that information stored in cyberspace is equivalent to the real knowledge held in the depth of our humanity and unfolded through the great tales of human endeavour, as revealed in our cultural histories.

According to some of our finest philosophers, especially Plato in the West and Shankara in the East, knowledge is the very essence of a human being and the very essence of every subject worth our attention. The character of a human being is the collection of his experiences over many lifetimes, and even if not everyone accepts the theory of human evolution or the transmigration of souls, most accept the law of cause and effect. We are the product of experience.

The person who can come to know the eternal principles of a subject, and that those principles are largely to be found in himself, has a right to claim some mastery of it. Plato's view is that knowledge is already complete in the human being and that the whole process of education is to bring it out – *educare.* That is not possible without the power of concentration. Shankara is of the view that the human being is quintessentially intelligent; that such intelligence has an innate ability to discern the temporal from the eternal and the real from the unreal. Knowing right from wrong and truth from falsehood is not a matter of collecting facts or information; it is a matter of true knowledge. Education, if it is to be worth anything substantial, is about accessing that ability.

Our examination system over recent years has systematically moved away from testing whether any principle is understood and focussed increasingly on the acquisition of facts and information. The consequence is that youngsters are asked to learn and digest countless facts in the belief that it is knowledge, something they find mindlessly boring to do because the information is inherently meaningless to them and it is far easier just to google it.

On an inset day at the start of the academic year, with a larger number of new teachers present than usual, I asked every teacher the following question: What is the magic in your subject? The responses were dynamic.

The mathematicians revealed that the magic in their subject lies in the number 1: every number is separated by 1, therefore, the number 1 must have an absolute power. 'I am Number One' is the call of the ego, and 'I am One' is the declaration of the wise, referring to God or the Absolute. The historians said the magic in their subject comes to life when they don't just impart facts, but rather, teach about humankind's trials, tribulations, and successes as a journey of consciousness. The biologists said the magic is revealed in the form of patterns repeated throughout the natural world, as well as in the laboratory. The physicists saw that there is enormous space pervading every material form, such that materiality hardly exists at all. The chemists saw an extraordinary lawfulness in all interactions, a lawfulness that is repeated in human interactions too. The linguists said that words are aspects of a cosmic vibration; that grammar is its lawful expression; and that the result of language and words is civilisation and culture. The magic was everywhere.

A real teacher, coping with the challenges of the future, will need to have the ability to look into the soul of his pupils and allow the inner revelation of that magic to occur. Head teachers of the future will need the confidence and courage to let teachers inspire their pupils in this way – the way of revelation of true knowledge, not acquisition of dull facts. Youngsters, with the power to concentrate and the ability to look into themselves to uncover the hidden gems of true knowledge and principle, will be the next generation of young leaders. Head teachers of the future will need to know how to guide them.

The first thing, which will be personal to each one of the next generation of heads, will be to evolve the ability to cope with mistakes and disasters. You may ask, why is this first? The answer is simple: mistakes and disasters are bound to happen! If the inner capacity of the new heads is not resolute and their personal mastery not strong enough, the job that needs doing will simply be left. It cannot afford to be.

For some time, going right back to my earliest mistakes and disasters, which in the great scheme of things didn't really matter to anyone other than me, I have used a simple catch phrase to help me maintain my equilibrium and keep going forward: 'If all this goes terribly wrong, will the Earth keep turning on its axis?' I would ask myself the question at the beginning, middle, or end of a leadership adventure, and sometimes repeatedly throughout the experience. As daft as the phrase might appear, it inevitably helped me to pull back from believing in the calamity, and because of that, the calamity never really happened. We do, indeed, think into existence our own crises.

I have observed, having talked to many deputies keen on headship, that it is their inner fear of failure and getting it wrong that stops them from stepping up to the job and doing what is needed. The state of our education is such that we cannot just have yes-men and women in these posts. We need educational adventurers who are prepared to see the real needs of the souls in front of them and, if necessary, throw over convention to meet them.

One of my personal heroes is Swami Vivekananda, who appeared out of the East at the turn of the twentieth century and wowed western audiences with the simple wisdom of his Vedantic tradition. 'What makes one man great and another weak is the difference in the faith he has in himself', he told his followers. (*Education: Extracts from Speeches & Writings of Swami Vivekananda*, page 17.)

Faith in oneself comes partly from experience but primarily from our inner ability to connect with a deeper peace and contentment beyond the surface of the mind. To do that requires in ourselves the ability to concentrate and to harness the enormous power of stillness, which is always present within us, but seldom accessed.

Throughout this book I have talked about meditative and reflective exercises and the benefits they bring, but greatest of all the benefits is this: faith in oneself. Faith gives the energy to do the job, to overcome the impediments, and to keep going.

Some may be surprised that I am saying faith in 'oneself' and not faith in the One God. Faith in God, for some, will be very important, but such faith will ultimately translate into faith in oneself. The stillness that concentration brings delivers the mind and heart into the centre of God-consciousness. It is an internal experience of being at peace, not an external reliance on another force.

Faith is harnessed by many things and, like any insurance policy, it needs to be in place before you call upon it. I try to make a daily habit of spending a few moments reorienting my intent (see chapter 5). This is just a quick inner review of the day – not checking whether my to-do list has been completed, but whether the work of the day has advanced my reason for being in the job: the uplift of the human condition. I don't spend too much time beating myself up on how slow the progress has been; there is enough ability to watch the movements of the mind and decide not to go in that direction. We all need to deepen our practice of becoming the Knower, the witness of all that is filling the mind and heart.

The greatest source of faith is connection with the Knower, that inner guide which is full of conscious power, intelligence, and love. Experience helps to distinguish when the Knower speaks, as well as when the ego speaks, laced as it is with self-criticism and negative commentary. Gentle assent from the inner Knower that the work has been good today creates a foundation of faith that is essential to call on when things do go wrong, as they inevitably will.

When things go wrong, not only does faith and self-belief give you strength to keep going and clear up the mess, but it also allows you to remember quickly that everything is in fact transitory. Today's negative headlines will wrap tomorrow's fish and chips, and the day after tomorrow they will be recycled. Of course, events that go wrong leave their mark on those they affect, but they need not leave an indelible mark on your own heart. A stick beating on a hard surface will scratch it and mark it forever, but a stick beating in water makes no lasting impression. Our hearts need to be like water, which they are when we are filled with faith and love of those in our care. If we take on the job to serve the needs we see in front of us, our hearts will have this fluidity; if we take on the job to massage our own egos, our hearts will have a hardness that will be scratched when disasters occur.

To arise to meet the educational challenges of the next decade and more, the next generation of headmasters and headmistresses will have to be extraordinary characters. Their hearts will need to be filled with love and compassion for the human condition around them. Their minds will need to be clear as to how to meet those challenges. They will certainly have to lead from behind. They will need to be fit and strong to keep going when every ounce of their body wants them to stop. They will need training in understanding human psychology and philosophy, not just in techniques of administration and health and safety.

I feel confident that such individuals will arise to take on the many jobs that await them. History has shown again and again how the divine forces have an unpredictable way of working to meet human needs. These men and women may not see themselves as great souls, but they are great within and great in the making: each is potentially divine in himself or herself, as Swami Vivekananda would say of those human beings who are called to work for the welfare of their fellow citizens.

I believe the call to take up headships has never been louder. At the same time, the paradox of our modern society has never been greater. We can put men on the moon and bring them safely back to Earth; we can tap numbers on pieces of plastic and speak to people at the other end of the world; we can map our DNA, and we can discover new galaxies and bigger blacker holes. But as a society we still cannot fathom how to live in peace and harmony. To do that, society needs proper teachers.

The ultimate teacher is one who dispels the darkness of ignorance; who brings hopes to the hearts and minds of people and sets them free to be themselves. This freedom is the birth right of every human being, and it goes along with his or her immortality.

The status in society of a teacher has never needed to be lifted more than it does today. A teacher who is called to do the work of the Divine is indeed responding to a vocation. When you know you have embarked on one of the greatest of vocations, because without your impulse of love and service other human beings will stay in misery and poverty, then the faith to cope with anything somehow makes itself manifest. Whatever happens as you try to break down the barriers of either prejudice or simple ignorance, you will need to know at the level of the Knower, at peace in your own heart, that the Earth will keep turning on its axis.

There is one final catch. The head's work of removing ignorance will never be complete. It will not be able to be tucked away neatly, allowing you to move on to new pastures. The head will always be looking out for the next generation of teachers, as well as what they need to know and how their emotional intelligence needs to mature to meet the demands before them. We are expected to help them see the needs and prepare them to give their very best to those in their care, just as we have tried to do.

The wisdom of the Bhagavad Geeta becomes a rock on which to go forward. Work, not for the sake of personal reward, but in the memory that it is the Divine's intelligence and power, coursing through us, which is doing everything. Follow that, and a deep satisfaction will be with you, every day.

# CHAPTER 13

# SUCCESS IN HEADSHIP: 7 PRINCIPLES OF EMOTIONAL INTELLIGENCE

THIS GUIDE HAS AIMED AT helping heads both survive and thrive in their jobs. I hope it has also inspired those considering the highest levels of school leadership to step forward and succeed in this work.

To measure success in school leadership is not easy. Conventional reference points can be applied, but they are limited. Real success is far more than the intense personal satisfaction that comes when a student acknowledges that your intervention made a difference to his or her life. It is far greater than showing how the school roll has swollen, or how the balance sheet has moved out of the red, or even how the school has risen in the league tables since you took over.

The successful head is the one who, whilst doing the job, has realised something utterly true about himself and used that inner knowledge as a foundation to improve the lives of those he serves and loves.

During my own headship there have been plenty of worldly successes, and various failures too. Both have helped me learn more about myself, perhaps the failures rather more than the successes. It has been a source of confidence to know that parents have wanted to send their children to the school where I have served as head because it delivered excellent growth of character and fine academic results. It is also comforting to know that the school is in far better shape, financially and in terms of its standing in the educational community, than it was when I arrived.

Although these things have happened, they have not provided the source of deep inner contentment that is so important for someone doing this job. Above all else, contentment and inner nourishment have come from the realisation that headship has given me the privilege of serving fellow human beings. Whether they think the job has been done well or not, a sense of success comes from knowing that you are on earth to serve others and, through that, allowing yourself and everyone else to grow in the fullness of love, intelligence, and knowledge. When you grow as a head, everyone around you has the chance to grow too – your pupils, your colleagues, and the parents.

From this it has been possible to set forth seven emotional intelligence principles that need to be in place to allow this self-growth to occur and become the source from which more growth arises. As heads we are universal gardeners: the seeds are our pupils, and their quality of character in our society will become known as the blossoming. Ultimately, those flowers will stand tall by themselves, but whilst they are young, we are the stakes standing beside them.

My belief is that every head and prospective head should aim to develop these seven emotional intelligence principles, creating a firm foundation from which their jobs – and their lives – can flourish.

## 1 Cultivating the Power of Awareness

Our awareness is our consciousness, and our consciousness is the source of all knowledge. When our awareness grows, the inner Knower discussed in this book stands strong. By 'growing' awareness, I mean growing the ability to connect with that awareness in the present moment. Simply knowing what is happening around you, with the colleagues and pupils you work with, is an invaluable help to keeping your vision intact.

No one else can grow your awareness; you have to do it yourself. Throughout this book there are exercises aimed at that development, accompanied, I hope, by motivation and inspiration. Awareness is actually always complete, but our connection with it can be disturbed.

Awareness allows detachment. This is not cold-heartedness; on the contrary, it inspires and allows the spirit of love to flow where it should, in the way it should. Detachment, however, also keeps you centred and unmoved when the vicissitudes of headship fall on you and threaten to knock you off your perch.

When a situation is clear it is because the power of the Knower is present. When a situation is uncertain or cloudy, the Knower has become covered. Just remaining with the power of awareness and watching, like an eternal witness, ultimately lets the clouds disperse. This watching is different from 'thinking things through'. That process often just puts more clouds in place. The recommended approach is to work from your inner or essential self first, because your inner self is full of consciousness, even if the ego mind says that it is not.

I was well into writing this book when I came under strong personal attack. The 'fighter' within me was raring to be let loose, but the quieter Knower held me back with the simple knowledge: 'Just watch events unfold. Do nothing but stay calm and remain totally awake and aware'. I had given that advice to so many others and seen it work. I now knew that, despite the provocation, it was the best advice for me in this situation too.

Sure enough, the less 'involved' I became and the more 'aware' of what was happening, the quieter things in the outer world became. In meditation one morning, I could see the problem and the perceptions around it, and dealing with it would now be relatively simple. I knew who to speak to, who to get advice from, who else to contact, and what to say, as well as what not to say. The Knower is always totally present and the power of awareness connects fully with it.

Staying in the present moment, remaining fully awake and aware, is the foundation from which every emotional intelligence principle unfolds. It is also the primary force in leadership of any kind, especially when the welfare of humanity is directly affected by it, as it is in headship.

## 2 Trusting Intuition

When the Knower communicates to the mind, it is just as often in the form of what we call intuition as it is in the form of fully-fledged ideas and concepts. Intuition is the Knower's shorthand; only when you follow it will you find out what it really is saying.

To trust your intuition takes courage and practice. My first mentor observed that I was sensitive to intuition and encouraged me to use it in dealing with the smallest of things, like knowing when somebody needed a cup of tea, and then providing it even before he or she asked. Of course, I got it wrong sometimes, but more often than not, the intuition proved accurate. From those small beginnings, I have come to trust these feelings, or 'emotional knowledges', more completely, and now I do not hesitate when the Knower puts a feeling or knowledge about something in my heart.

We can sometimes think of intuition as a rather haphazard affair; that it just turns up, and if it does, it might be interesting to follow. When you start to trust it, however, you will find the startling fact that intuition is nearly always present and available, so long as you have the courage to follow it. It is like a platform from which responses can emerge. It can often be recognised when events require very speedy responses: it has a response on the instant and then unfolds itself as you start to follow it. Intuition is often the key to leading events by following them.

Intuition contains the seed form of knowledge, which is why it is not always clear to the mind what is happening, at least at first. A parent arrived in our reception wanting to see his son and yet intuition clearly called for caution. So we followed that. A few phone calls later, we determined that he had come to the school from the divorce courts, angered by a judgement against him. He loved his son, but his anger could well have taken itself out on the boy. The intuition to be cautious and actually to protect the boy from his father turned out to be right.

The intuitive leader has often been portrayed as a risk-taker, but only by those who are fearful and averse to risk. Why would seeing something clearly from deep within, even if no one else can see it, be a risk? In fact, it is the opposite of risky; it eliminates uncertainty and gives the leader the chance to progress.

Some leadership models portray intuition as a power that needs 'controlling'. This is not what I am advocating. My advice is to seek to 'harness' it – to cultivate the use of it. It will enable the leader to know when he is being lied to or when he is not getting the whole truth. This power, more than most, will assist the third principle of emotional intelligence, *being fearless*, to unfold naturally and easily.

## 3  Being Fearless

Fearlessness can be cultivated as a state of being, simply by being fearless.

Fearlessness can be talked about, and it is often on leadership development courses. But no imagined experience of terror or fear can be anything like the real thing, which shakes our inner core when it arrives.

We live in a world pervaded by fear. We fear our bodies and property will be damaged, our wealth taken away, and our reputation destroyed if we make mistakes. Fear turns out to be a matter of the emotions, which need to be handled using both mental and spiritual means.

Spiritual teachers tell the story of the man who enters a dark room and suddenly freezes. Standing near the door is a thief with a hatchet. In blind panic, the man lunges for the light switch. The beam of light reveals that the 'thief with a hatchet' was merely a coat stand with hats on it! Light always dispels darkness: awareness and intuition always dispel fear.

The mental constructs we create when a difficulty arises feed the fear within us. What we have to come to see is that fear is born in the darkness of ignorance, not the light of knowledge. Being fearless means not allowing the mind to dwell in areas that are simply not good for it.

A young colleague, scheduled to be observed by an inspector, could not get out of her mind the fear associated with it; she was petrified even when her senior colleagues sat in on her lessons. She would commence every formal lesson observation with the idea that all her faults would be revealed, and so, inevitably, she did silly things that she would never normally do. Finally, when it all became too much for her, she asked for help.

'Just decide not to allow the mind to go there', I advised. 'Turn the mind away and think of something else.'

After several months of trying to do this, she became increasingly aware of how the mind tumbled around without direction. Then suddenly she saw that where it went was a matter of choice.

'Now I know I can choose where to place my mind and the attention', she told me during a review.

'Yes, perfect!' I said.

The practice for her in being fearless was not to allow the mind to dwell in areas that would cause her pain and distress.

One of the main causes of fear is the worry about 'what people think of me!' It is possible for this idea to dominate all the waking hours of a school head. Being fearless requires evolving a personal method to deal with this; thus the idea, 'If all this goes wrong, the Earth will still keep turning on its axis.' (See chapter 12.) The head who worries about what people think of him will ultimately sink in a self-induced swamp of mental crocodiles. Don't let the mind go there.

Fearlessness creates stability, which comes from a deepening appreciation of harmony, compassion, and Oneness. If you can come to see that even the most difficult character is worthy of respect; that understanding someone's nature and make-up often means realising he can't be different from what he is; that ultimately, we all share the same spirit as part of the human family, you will experience the practice of being fearless.

Cultivating the power of *awareness* naturally supports *trusting your intuition*, which in turn sustains *being fearless*. These are the first three emotional intelligence principles that the head needs to nourish for survival.

The next three principles create the emotional atmosphere for the head to flourish, and the final one holds all of them together.

## 4 Practising Inter-dependency

An early mentor once told me that my inability to receive help was evidence of my ego. I had not seen that I depended on him just as he depended on me. It was not the basic human kind of dependency: I did not need him to help feed my family or provide anything in the material world. It was the emotional dependency that comes with any community or society.

We are utterly inter-dependent on each other and on the universe itself. What might be a new idea is that inter-dependency can be 'practised' and the more it is acknowledged and deliberately executed, the more the space opens up around an action. The greater the space, the more the inherent emotional intelligence can arise, and the greater the vision of Oneness.

Who is more dependent on whom? The mother or the child? The teacher or the pupil? The policeman or the thief? The doctor or the patient? The world is in fact full of these inter-dependencies, but we sit on one side of the fence and forget that our being depends on the chap on the other side.

It may appear to you as a head that a large number of people depend on you: governors, pupils, staff, and parents, not to mention the officialdom of inspectors, advisers, examiners, and health and safety experts! If you were not there, they could not do their job, yet if they were not there, you could not do yours either.

Practising inter-dependency involves curbing criticisms, curbing damnations, and giving thanks inwardly, even for the most awkward of people or situations. In the midst of suffering the sustained personal attack mentioned above, I turned over my daily calendar, which has helpful quotes from my guide Swami Vivekananda. His words read, 'Bless people when they revile you. Think how much good they are doing by helping to stamp out the false ego'. Now, that is real inter-dependency!

When you come to know as a truth that your own role is utterly dependent on those around you, it is far easier to become a 'servant-leader'. In a way, it becomes true self-service. You are serving those on whom you depend and allowing them to serve the self in you too. Those who serve create an ever greater space for their being; those who just look after themselves and miss the inter-dependency end up in a far smaller and less happy world of their own creation.

Somehow, spotting the inter-dependencies in any situation helps you to step back from it, see the tragedy or humour in it, just as in a theatre play, and stop wishing it were different. It allows acceptance, which itself provides the ground for further awareness, intuition, and fearlessness regarding what to do next. It also keeps you fluid and responsive to following events. It allows the philosophy of Oneness to become a reality.

## 5  Keeping Fluid

The emotionally intelligent leader knows how to stay fluid, which means he does not get bound by either difficulties or sticky relationships. He is capable of moving on with the events. He feels confident he has the right leadership 'clubs' with which to face any situation (see chapter 7), and he knows how to play them. If he bungles a shot, he will not throw in the towel; if he scores a hole in one, he will not stop the game to party before the work is finished.

One of our greatest pitfalls is taking things too personally. If it hasn't gone right 'it must be my fault' is the common refrain, yet when we share our stories of a difficult day, we usually find that nearly everyone has had a difficult time of some sort. The reason for that is the energies in the universe (the *gunas*) are unbalanced, pushing everything out of kilter. The approach has to be to release oneself and stay fluid; to empty the mind and rest in the pure awareness, just watching.

This particular emotional intelligence principle has far-reaching consequences. The leader who can stay fluid and meet all kinds of events with a consistent evenness, not allowing things to stick, may be misunderstood by some, but more often than not engenders fierce loyalty from those who recognise in him the quality of being unshakable. He tends to generate great confidence in his supporters and allows others to be at ease in his presence.

The fluid leader cultivates a warm heart, and empathy comes naturally to him – but he will not suffer fools. He tends to be less stressful, and as a consequence, his social skills allow him to move in and out of situations without tension. The remark often made is that he is 'always even', no matter what is being faced. This can be of tremendous value, especially when crises and difficulties present themselves, which they inevitably do. If he has to deal with difficult people or those who oppose him, he will demonstrate clarity and certainty of action and then move on from whatever the result turns out to be.

The opposite of the fluid leader is the one who takes everything utterly seriously and personally. It is as if his own future depends on what will happen next, and whatever does happen seems to scar him, like a huge scratch across his hardened heart. The hard heart is uncomfortable to live with and makes living peacefully nearly impossible for everyone else.

The key to staying fluid is to exercise the practise of letting go or emptying one's mind. To gain a sense of what this involves, hold out your right hand and clench the fist for a few seconds. Now release the clench. That is letting go. The more you keep letting go, the greater the emptying process.

Letting go in the mind is like unclenching the fist. You see (due to the power of awareness) the idea appear and then you let it go. It is just like letting clouds pass in the sky.

When people try this, they sometimes talk about the thoughts coming back to haunt them, but soon they start to see that another set of ideas is operating, sending those unhelpful thoughts back: 'I can't do without this' and 'but surely I am needed here' are examples. Let go again and keep watching.

The fluid leader's space in which to operate seems to grow inexorably. The more fluid he is, the more empathetic and loving he is. The greater the challenge, perhaps from a colleague using the pacesetter club (see chapter 7), the gentler his general response and the smoother the outcome. Remaining fluid is crucial for the utilization of all the leadership clubs. As a golfer will tell you, the easiest of shots becomes more difficult the tighter you grip the club. Remaining fluid keeps the swinging of all the leadership clubs smooth but decisive, for the benefit of all.

## 6  Believing in Self – Believing in Others

No matter how strong colleagues, friends, mentors, or family can be, the head who does not believe in himself is going to struggle. And no matter how accommodating or generous a head is, he cannot get done what needs doing without believing in the right people around him. Getting them on his bus is a matter of exercising emotional intelligence.

This principle is the easiest to misread or misinterpret. Self-belief is frequently mistaken for belief that those with the biggest egos make the best leaders. They don't. The head, however, who humbly understands the enormity of the task ahead of him yet is fiercely resolved to tread daily through the forest of the job, chop down the thorn bushes, and find the promised land where his vision of human potential can prosper – such a head is certain to succeed. Such a head will also know, often through pure awareness and intuition, who should be on the bus with him and who will have the communication and emotional intelligence skills to get there. In the largest sense of the term, self-belief is a belief in that which is essential to the self in us all. That is our common consciousness and creativity, the brilliance of the Knower. Knowing that the Knower can be relied upon allows humility and keeps the ego at bay. It gives the strength to know that the ego is not in charge of things, that there is a greater force at play, and that events can be followed.

Belief in others is belief that the Knower is in them too. Their personalities and issues may be different from yours, but they are powered by the same conscious presence. This does not mean every one of your colleagues deserves the right to sit on the bus with you, but it does mean that every one of them has a talent and capacity to contribute, and when they do, deserves your respect, even if you cannot bring it upon yourself to actually like them. Such an approach goes a long way towards implementing an environment of Oneness.

Oneness as an approach to leadership is not the romantic notion that all differences between people either disappear or are ignored as if for the sake of the greater good. It is a subtle opening of the emotional intelligence to embrace everyone for who he or she is, to recognise individuals for their talents and foibles, and to help them find a way to make their contribution. It also involves finding ways for them to leave when that contribution is done, even if they don't know it.

I have always cherished Swami Vivekananda's proposition that every person is 'potentially divine'. It allows even the most difficult of characters to be given a chance. It means the divine spark that many philosophers tell us is in every person has the opportunity – and ability - to be fully lit. With that vision, a community in the school can unfold as an assemblage of lights, each of whom burns a little differently in shape, hue, and intensity, but whose common feature is their power to shine. From the standpoint of emotional intelligence, this is diametrically opposed to the idea that every person is potentially troublesome.

One of my senior colleagues wrote to our Chairman of Governors, outlining all the qualities of leadership he had seen in the several head teachers he had worked for in his forty-year career. One, he said, had failed under the sway of the whisky bottle; another had been a social pariah; a third had resolutely failed to connect or communicate because he could not easily see the potential good in colleagues or pupils. The very best heads, he declared, were those who had an unshakeable belief in the people around them and the ability to communicate a vision of how that belief could manifest.

This principle is not only the easiest to misinterpret; it is also the easiest to cloud over with the pale cast of thought. The daily reality is that we are always thinking about our colleagues, in one way or another. Hardly a day goes by without my mental exercising about the inner condition of colleagues, those closest to my work as well as those sitting in a corner of the staffroom. I readily admit to frustration with those corner-hugging sceptics and there have been days when I thought the divine authority had passed them by when he placed Himself in the hearts of us all. Practising this principle of belief in others as an emotional intelligence exercise means having time to take stock on a regular basis; to reconnect with the essence of each person, even silently in your own mind.

I asked a head teacher over dinner how she coped with difficult staff, the ones who seem to be at the centre of every ounce of staff discontent. She looked up from her meal, put down her knife and fork and calmly told me, 'I pray for them, and I pray that I may get the strength to look after them, just as I do my own family'. Before I expressed my disbelief, I caught myself and stopped, fortunately. She really meant what she had said.

Whether the inclination is to pray or just to inwardly consider, the practice is a good one, because it reconnects all to the whole so the sense of Oneness can prevail again within you, and probably in the staffroom too. This in turn helps to restore self-belief should it have been covered up, as an after-effect of the events of the day. The energy to do this on a regular basis is significantly helped by simply remaining cheerful.

## 7 Remaining Cheerful

This principle is so easy to pass over, and yet it is the glue that holds everything together. Cheerfulness keeps people together as our mutual dependency becomes ever more obvious, as does the importance of believing in yourself and in the potential of all others.

Plenty about headship generates frustration, anxiety, and even anger. Cheerfulness is the antidote to deal with it all. No matter what is before you, a few conscious deep breaths and putting on the countenance of a delightful cheerfulness will somehow wipe away all doubts and regenerate your energy, enabling you to meet what is there with the fullness of emotional intelligence. The habit of walking around the school with a cheerful half-smile fills others with the same energy. Furthermore, the half-smile on your face will transform your own inner gremlins faster and more efficiently than any external mechanism such as anti-depressant pills or a lunch time glass of wine.

There is no doubting the extraordinary level of demand placed on the head's inner resources. The role is utterly relentless and yet completely fulfilling if you can find the way to manage your emotions and responses. This book has emerged because traditional training of heads has not really dealt with what it is like on the ground, day after day, coping with the stuff of humankind. So many of the children we have to care for come from unhappy families. So many of our colleagues face challenges to their self-esteem and sense of self-worth, both of which can be knocked for six after a bad lesson or two with 9M. The classic school leaders' manual talks about cultivating good and supportive relationships with your governors and other school managers, but the reality all too often is that these crucial relationships are extremely strained. Headship can be very lonely.

The essence of all emotional intelligence, according to its acknowledged guru, Daniel Goleman, is self-knowledge. In the context of this book, it means the head has himself to turn to, first and last, as the most reliable support in all circumstances. But this only means something if he gets to know himself through practising these emotional intelligence principles.

The companionship of other heads doing similar tasks, found in the various heads' organisations and societies, is invaluable and should be availed frequently, especially by the new head or the person thinking of taking on the role. The support of loved ones and families too can be most important, but then sometimes the toll of the job is felt most painfully by the family. Once you come to know yourself, however, you will never feel unsupported.

If a head has found the secret of staying cheerful and practises it even when all the circumstances around him are otherwise, then he has found the elixir of headship – perhaps even life itself.

Life insurance actuaries recently presented to The Society of Heads the startling news that head teachers who retire at around sixty have a life expectancy of another twenty-seven years; those who retire at sixty-five have a life expectancy of around eighteen months. Whether or not that is accurate, it certainly got many of us thinking! Now in my sixtieth year, I am inclined to take the hint.

Headship is an extraordinary opportunity for a man or woman to make a difference to the lives of countless souls. I did not choose to enter headship; through events it appeared to choose me. I suspect it has been the same for the vast majority of the many extraordinary men and women I have met who have also been doing this task and playing this part.

Not many people understand what calls headship makes on the human psyche – perhaps only those currently in the job and those who have retired from it do. Even very close colleagues sometimes cannot see what happens when your door closes behind you and only you are there, doing your very best to serve the needs of the human beings in your care.

I have felt enormously privileged serving as a head. There is no better calling than to find yourself and to be truly useful to the human family. This call comes from the Divine. My advice therefore to prospective heads is to heed it. You will regret nothing and gain everything. Especially yourself.